Freedom of Infor

PHILOSOPHY AND IMPLEMENTATION

Proceedings of the Conference on Freedom of Information, Dublin, November 1997 organised by the Government Libraries Section of the Library Association of Ireland

edited by

JOSEPH DONNELLY AND MARY DOYLE

on behalf of the GLS

General Editor

CLAIRE ROURKE

BLACKHALL
Publishing

This book was typeset by
Gough Typesetting Services for
BLACKHALL PUBLISHING
26 Eustace Street
Dublin 2

e-mail: blackhall@tinet.ie

ISBN: 1 901657 37 X

A catalogue record for this book
is available from the British Library.

Printed in Ireland by
Betaprint.

CONTENTS

FOREWORD

THE BACKGROUND

The Conference on Freedom of Information, at which these papers were first presented, on 12 November 1997 was organised by the Government Libraries Section of the Library Association of Ireland and, in particular, by Michael O'Gorman, Librarian in the State Laboratory, Abbotstown, Dublin. All of the Committee members of the GLS helped in organising the event, and it was my pleasure to chair it. I co-edited these proceedings with Mary Doyle, Chair of the Government Libraries Section of the LAI and Librarian in the Department of Agriculture and Food and who, I must confess, carried much more than her fair share of the burden in the editing process. Other members of the Committee who merit special mention for their efforts are Lisa Shields (Met Éireann), Valerie Ingram (Office of Public Works) and Carol Flynn (Department of Enterprise, Trade & Employment).

In recent years it has become traditional for the Government Libraries Section of the LAI and the government librarians in Northern Ireland to have an annual joint meeting, and 'freedom of information' was chosen as a topic that would be of interest to both groups, since the Act had just been passed in the Republic and legislation on the same area is currently under consideration in the UK. The subject was, of course, of interest to many others as well as librarians, and the Conference was attended by well over a hundred people – a capacity audience – including civil servants, academics and interested members of the public, as well as librarians, among whom was the group of government librarians from Northern Ireland.

That the Conference was deemed a success (and was accessible at a charge, which was nominal, to cover refreshments) was due to the generosity of the speakers in giving of their time and expertise, and to the financial sponsorship provided by EBSCO Information Services, Lendac Data Systems Ltd, the legal publishers Round Hall Sweet & Maxwell and Hodges Figgis bookshop. The Office of Public Works kindly made available the Coach House of Dublin Castle, in the heart of Dublin. It was a particularly attractive venue in a historic setting, the Castle having been the centre of administration in Ireland for several centuries before independence. In addition, the Castle Garden – or Dubh Linn Garden – beside the Coach House, marks the site of the ancient tidal Black Pool, which in former times extended from the Liffey, and beside which sprung up one of the two settlements which were the dual origins of Dublin; indeed this Black Pool or Dubh Linn gave its name to Dyflin or Dublin.

Last, but by no means least, the success of the Conference owed a great deal to the interest shown by all who attended, and, in many cases, participated in the discussion after the formal papers.

THE PAPERS

Senator Brendan Ryan was the most appropriate person to deliver the opening address, given his long-standing interest in the subject he introduced a Bill on Freedom of Information in 1988. He welcomes, with some reservations, the Act of 1997 as revolutionary, while pointing out that it is one part (though a very thorough one) of a continuous process, which will include the extension of the application of the Act and a change in attitudes within public bodies.

Niall Michel was not a speaker at the Conference, but he kindly offered a paper for distribution, and it is reproduced in this collection, providing a concise, but useful, overview of the Act and its implications, while also mentioning practical difficulties which have been encountered in implementing similar legislation in Canada.

Gerry Kearney, who heads the Freedom of Information Central Policy Unit in the Department of Finance, sets the Act, and its philosophy, in the context of wider reform in public life. He provides a detailed outline of the implementation of the Act, as well as discussing its impact on public administration and on the citizen.

It was to be expected that **Eithne Fitzgerald** would be enthusiastic about the Act, since, as Minister of State at the Office of the Tánaiste, she steered the Bill along its path to enactment – a path that was not without obstacles. However, far from delivering a vague statement of support for openness, she showed her deeply felt commitment to a radical re-engineering of the way decision-making is undertaken in public administration. Her enthusiasm was infectious, and equally impressive were her familiarity with each provision of the Act and her interest in the practical workings of the new system. Indeed, her main theme concerns "the next steps" that are necessary after enactment. She emphasises in her paper, as she did in answer to questions from the floor, that the Act creates positive duties, thereby assisting citizens to know of the relevant information available to them and to make this information available appropriately and without delay.

Maeve McDonagh has made quite a study of freedom of information legislation in various jurisdictions and she assesses the possible impact of the

Irish Act by looking at related legislation in Australia, Canada and New Zealand, comparing the scope of the Acts, the exemptions and enforcement measures.

Dr Paschal Preston sets the Freedom of Information Act in the broader context of citizenship information in Europe and the role of technology in providing access to governmental information, touching also on moves to promote the sale of government-generated information. He looks at various aspects of citizenship information needs, including information related to rights and services, as well as accountability and participation. This embraces not only information technology and face-to-face expert advice, but also the commercialisation of information supply (where a "market" can be identified) and the effects of poverty, disability and other disadvantages, which influence both the need for information and access to it. Among his conclusions, he identifies the importance of public policy initiatives in information by national governments and by the EU.

Roy Atkinson, with his perspective as Vice-Chairman of the Consumers' Association of Ireland, looks at difficulties which may confront citizens as both information subjects and information consumers, drawing on past experience related to the way information issues have been handled in the context of the Data Protection Act, the planning process, and the Directive on Access to Environmental Information. Issues that have concerned him in the past include: identifying the relevant information, knowing where to find it, one's bargaining power and pressure to contract out of one's right to privacy, the cost of accessing information and the difficulties which can arise in obtaining copies. He concludes that the utility of this welcome piece of legislation will depend on how it is operated.

Bernadette Kennedy's paper reminds us that the time does not simply become ripe for an idea. The final outcome and its precise nature are influenced by factors, which arise at a very early stage, including the definition of a problem, the agendas (and resources) of various groups, their influence on policy-makers and decisions about which proposals to consider and which to drop. She shows how events, and decisions, in Ireland in the 1990s gave rise to the current legislation.

This leads neatly to the paper of **Michael Foley**, media correspondent of *The Irish Times*. While he is generally very positive about the Act, as a radical step designed to end a culture of secrecy, he nevertheless concentrates on a shift in emphasis towards a private right to information, rather than a public right to transparent government. He lists, among the issues not dealt with in the Act, a "whistle-blower's charter" (implementation of which has been delayed), cabinet confidentiality and changes in areas of the law of particular interest to the media, such as the right to keep secret a journalist's sources of information and the law of defamation.

All told, this is a varied and thought-provoking collection of papers, which I hope you will find as interesting as I have. They are accompanied here by the full text of the Act, the Explanatory and Financial Memorandum of the Bill and a select bibliography.

Joseph Donnelly, Conference Chairman
Librarian, The Judges' Library, Dublin

January 1999

LIST OF SPONSORS

Conference on Freedom of Information

The conference was generously supported by the following sponsors:

Hodges Figgis, the Bookstore
Dawson Street
Dublin 2
Ireland
Telephone: +353 (0)1 677 4754
Fax: +353 (0)1 677 4939
Web Site: http://www.hodgesfiggis.com
Email: Queries@HFiggis.ie

EBSCO Information Services
1 Mill Street
London SE1 2DF
UK
Telephone: +44 (0)171 2370444
Fax: +44 (0)171 2313393
Web Site: http://www.ebsco.com
Email: JBradley@EBSCO.COM

Lendac Data Systems
Unit 6, IDA Enterprise Centre
Pearse Street
Dublin 2
Ireland
Telephone: +353 (0)1 677 6133
Fax: +353 (0)1 671 0135
Web Site: http://kol/18367k
Email: marketing@lendac.ie

Round Hall Sweet & Maxwell
Legal Publishers,
4 Upper Ormond Quay
Dublin 7
Ireland
Telephone: +353 (0)1 873 0101
Fax: +353 (0)1 872 0078

The Committee of the Government Libraries Section of the LAI is very grateful to our sponsors for their help in enabling us to hold the conference.

The Committee would also like to thank the *Office of Public Works* for making the Coach House at Dublin Castle available as the conference venue.

There are links to the conference sponsor's web pages from the Freedom of Information Conference page: http://www.hea.ie/gls/index.html.

CHAPTER 1

OPENING ADDRESS: BUILDING A SOCIETY OF FREE INFORMATION

Senator Brendan Ryan*

This Act is of immense constitutional significance. It is a magnificent revolutionary piece of legislation and shows in its complexity all the signs of heavy resistance from within the political establishment. It is full of language which reflects a political determination that administrative guile would not be allowed to undermine the spirit of openness.

The Act is, therefore, hard work for the reader. It is a complex network of subclauses, forward references and backward references. It contains some of the most obscure language I have ever seen in legislation and also uses language that often appears inconsistent if not downright contradictory. The use of the imperative "shall" in some sections and the enabling "may" in other sections is particularly confusing.

But it is nevertheless a major innovation; even if it is only one part of a necessary revolution. I welcome, in particular, its especially prescriptive thoroughness. For instance it lists 36 Acts which contain "confidential information" clauses and insists that such clauses cannot be used to inhibit use of the Act. The Environmental Protection Agency Act contains a blanket prohibition on the disclosure of "confidential information", with "confidential information" being defined as any information which the EPA decides is confidential. The FOI Act ends that nonsense. Only information exempt under the FOI Act can be withheld by the EPA. It is the same for FÁS, for the Health and Safety Authority and many other agencies.

The Act also contains some extraordinary admonitions to the courts. Section 43 effectively wags a finger at the courts and warns them not to leak exempt information. I await their Lordships' reaction. A similar admonition is addressed to the Information Commissioner.

The Act is of course not perfect. For instance, it provides for non-disclosure of information which is commercially sensitive, or obtained in confi-

*Senator Brendan Ryan is a Senator in the Oireachtas. He introduced the first Freedom of Information Bill in 1988. He is author of *Keeping Us in the Dark: Censorship and Freedom of Information in Ireland* (Gill & Macmillan, 1995).

dence. It does however, allow, disclosure in exceptional circumstances. These are if "in the opinion" of the appropriate person "the public interest would be better served" by disclosure. Unfortunately, opinions are subjective things not open to challenge before the courts or Information Commissioners. It's a peculiar lapse from the Act's high standards of transparency and accountability.

The restrictions on disclosure of information on security-related matters are as one would expect. So is the obvious determination that the final decisions on these matters be kept away from the courts or the Information Commission. Only the Department of Justice could have thought up such a procedure. The arrogant assumption that "no one can be trusted except us" defies comment. But it appears to me they missed something. They have lost the blanket unchallengeable and unaccountable exemption they gave themselves in the Data Protection Act – progress indeed! Nevertheless the FOI Act is still revolutionary in intent and in its impact; but it's only a start and we will have to wait and see how it is extended beyond government departments, Local Authorities and Health Boards. We await a timetable.

Like all reforms it also exposes contradictions elsewhere. It will ultimately require unprecedented disclosure of information by bodies such as FÁS, the HSA, EPA, IDA, etc. But they will continue to do all their business behind closed doors. FÁS spends over £500 million of taxpayers' money every year, yet its Board meets in private. With FOI, much of its documentation will become public. The same should happen to its meetings. This could be the case in the US, where all Federal Agencies must meet in public when discussing anything which is not exempted from the United States' FOI Act. "Informal" meetings are included, as well as telephone conferences, etc. Furthermore all discussions between Agency and interested parties must be a matter of public record. Yet the skies have not fallen in the last twenty years.

Logic dictates it. Only expediency or something to hide could prevent it. There is more of course. Privatisation or semi-privatisation is on the cards for many State bodies. As this happens they will pass from a regime of optimum openness to one of maximum secrecy. Irish company law is secretive in the extreme. This prevents shareholders and the public from finding out about the environmental policy, the employment policy, or indeed the payment to directors and executives of such companies. Power shifts from the State to the private sector. Secrecy will return. We will be excluded. Consistency demands that we end this secrecy. Otherwise we are only exchanging one barrier for another.

Let us hope that the spirit of the FOI Act will inspire all public bodies. More and more of them have web pages so, when they are organised, why not put all their indices on the Web? Why not let us know what records have been made public and what areas are regarded as public? Let us re-write our law then to make access via the internet an equal, encouraged and cost-free way of allowing us our rights.

Finally, we can only regret the fact that the Act has limited retrospective force. Hopefully, good sense will prevail and the last 30 years will also be made known to us. Otherwise some independent senator might have to introduce amending legislation.

CHAPTER 2

TOWARDS GREATER GOVERNMENTAL TRANSPARENCY: THE FREEDOM OF INFORMATION ACT 1997

Niall Michel*

Between the idea
And the reality
Between the motion
And the act
Falls the shadow

The Hollow Men, T S Eliot

Freedom of information legislation is not a new concept to common lawyers. Rights of access to information have, for example, been enshrined in the laws of Canada, New Zealand and Australia since the early 1980s. By appending her signature on 21 April 1997 to the Freedom of Information Act 1997, the then President, Mary Robinson, saw in what is potentially an exciting new era of transparent government in this State.

This article does not purport to set out or examine in exhaustive detail the provisions of the Act but rather to give a general flavour of the rights and duties contained in it and to speculate as to what is likely to attend its future operation. There is also some brief comparative commentary on the equivalent piece of legislation in Canada.

The extent of the cultural change which will be caused by the coming into operation of the Act should not be underestimated, nor should the level of resources in terms of time and money, and the extensive potential for reviews and challenges regarding the Act itself or decisions made thereunder, be misjudged. The Act is a substantial piece of legislation, the implementation of

---

***Niall Michel** is a barrister and is now specialising and advising clients in the area of administrative law at Mason Hayes & Curran, Solicitors.

which will require significant effort. In consequence, provision is made for the Minister for Finance to make regulations to ensure that any difficulties in bringing the Act into operation are minimised (including regulations which modify provisions of the Act).

From April 1998, the Act confers three rights on members of the public. First, it confers a general right (known as "the right of access") to records held by public bodies. Secondly, it confers a right to the alteration or deletion of personal information in a record held by a public body where that record contains incomplete, incorrect or misleading information. And thirdly, it confers a right on a person, affected by an act of a public body in which he has a material interest, to obtain a statement in writing from the body as to (a) the reasons for the act and (b) any findings on any material issues of fact made for the purposes of the act.

The Act provides a comprehensive definition of what is comprised within the expression 'record'.

It would appear worthwhile, at this point, to make five practical points to correct likely misconceptions which prospective users of the Act might harbour. First, the reason or reasons for making a request for access to a record will be irrelevant to the question of whether or not such a request is granted. Secondly, the records to which access may be granted are not limited to those which relate to the requester (note that there are detailed provisions protecting privacy also). Thirdly, access may be granted under the Act only to records created after April 1998 (with certain exceptions, including where access to records created beforehand is necessary or expedient in order to understand records created after commencement and where access is requested to personal information relating to the requester). Fourthly, access to records may be sought and given in a variety of ways. And finally, a fee may be charged by the body to the requester.

It is also important to note that not all public bodies are within the ambit of the Act nor, indeed, are all records held by bodies which are within its ambit necessarily accessible under the right of access.

The First Schedule to the Act lists the bodies which are included and the Act empowers the Minister for Finance, amongst other things, to bring additional public bodies under the freedom of information regime and to prescribe the extent of the application of the regime to such bodies. The bodies listed at present include: government departments, the Offices of the Tánaiste, the Attorney General, the Director of Public Prosecutions and the Comptroller and Auditor General and certain, specified bodies or agencies such as the Revenue Commissioners, the Planning Appeals Board, the Competition Authority and (of recent, topical interest) the Blood Transfusion Service Board.

As regards the breadth of records which are accessible under the Act, one would have to acknowledge that no right of access can be unlimited and the Act provides for extensive limitations to the right, subject, in some cases, to the overriding criterion of the "public interest". Records which are not subject to this override include records concerning government meetings, public safety, law enforcement, security, defence and international relations. In a provision, which is potentially constitutionally infirm, a Minister of the government may certify conclusively that certain records concerning certain of the above-mentioned matters are exempt and therefore not accessible. The Act does not apply at all to certain, specified records, such as records held by the courts or a tribunal of inquiry or relating to an investigation or examination carried out by the Ombudsman (with certain exceptions).

Apart from the observance of the rights of requesters for access to records, the Act also provides for complementary duties on public bodies. For example, there is a duty to give reasonable assistance to persons seeking records under the Act in order to ensure that such persons do not stumble at procedural hurdles, such as the mode of making a request for access. There is a further duty to ensure that persons with disabilities are not placed at any disadvantage as regards the exercise of their rights under the Act. There is also an obligation to keep to certain deadlines (which may be extended and/or deferred) an obligation to give reasons for any refusal of access and a duty, upon application, to review decisions taken by them in relation to access to records.

Public bodies are also required, every three years, to prepare, publish and make available reference books containing a general description of their structure and organisation, functions, powers and duties, services provided for the public and the procedures under which such services are made available. In addition, bodies under the Act's umbrella must publish a general description of the classes of records held by them and of the manner in which they arrive at their decisions relating to matters affecting members of the public, together with appropriate information relating to the manner, or intended manner, of such bodies' administration of the enactment or scheme being administered by them. Further, the Act requires the relevant bodies to publish the arrangements made by them to enable persons to exercise certain rights provided for in the Act. These reference books should also contain names and designations of the members of the staff of the body responsible for carrying out these arrangements, appropriate information concerning any rights of review or appeal in respect of decisions made by the body (including rights of review and appeal under the Act) and the procedure governing the exercise of such rights and any time limits involved. A summary of each body's reference book is to be furnished to the Minister for Finance, who is to collate all the summaries so furnished and publish them in a reference book.

The Act grants a right to apply for a review to persons aggrieved by a variety of decisions taken by relevant public bodies. In the first instance, application may be made to the public body for a review, followed, if necessary, by an application to the Information Commissioner established by the Act, whose decision is binding (subject to appeal on a point of law to the High Court). The functions and powers of the Commissioner generally are extensive and include: keeping the operation of the Act under review, carrying out investigations into the practices and procedures of public bodies as regards the Act, publishing commentaries on the practical application and operation of the Act and preparing annual reports in relation to his activities under the Act.

What lies in store for the Irish freedom of information regime is difficult to prophesy, but the experiences of other jurisdictions with similar laws are likely to point the way. Observing the example of Canada, where the Access to Information Act has been on the statute books since 1983, it is possible to foresee many interesting benefits and shortcomings arising in Ireland. The Canadian Act shares many common provisions with the Irish Act, including a provision requiring the Canadian Information Commissioner to publish annual reports, setting out the activities of his office each year. These make fascinating reading, particularly when one considers that the operation of the legislation in this jurisdiction may develop in a similar way.

Whilst it is outside the scope of this article to delve into the minutiae of the Canadian experience since 1983, some general experiences may be relayed here in the hope of providing a snapshot of the future.

In Canada there was the initial problem of a widespread lack of awareness among the general public of the existence of the freedom of information law and a misunderstanding of the role of the Information Commissioner and these factors, when combined with a palpable distaste for the same on the part of public bodies, led to a slow start for the Canadian Act. The culture in the Canadian public service also had to be converted from that of holding an embedded belief in the need for secrecy to a willingness to provide as much information as was accessible under the law. Despite some gradual amelioration of the situation, these problems are still being encountered.

Other problems encountered include: public bodies looking for reasons not to give access rather than the other way around, delays in furnishing information, leverage being applied by public bodies by means of the selection of expensive forms of access to records, or specifying high search, retrieval and copy charges and invitations to narrow the scope of requests, imprecise framing of requests leading to refusals of access or greater expense than might have been necessary, sluggish procedures limiting the effectiveness of access to information rights in certain cases and high administration, training and compliance costs on the one hand and budget cutbacks on the other.

On the positive side, the Canadian Act has led to foreseeable but, perhaps, unforeseen benefits such as: the encouragement of public servants to be more precise in exercising their functions and performing their duties, the promotion of fiscal sobriety on the basis that disclosure of insobriety by means of the freedom of information law will cause embarrassment and the advancement of good government generally.

By far the biggest users of the Act in Canada are businesses seeking, in the main, to gather accessible intelligence. Frequent use of the law is also made by journalists and authors who use it as a research tool. Other individuals will use it for a variety of reasons, including its use as an adjunct to discovery in court proceedings (although if the delays which have been endemic in Canada replicate themselves here, this may not prove a useful device).

It is probably safe to say, in conclusion, that the Freedom of Information Act will take its place amongst the landmark statutes passed by our legislature since independence and will, in due course, lead to a major change in the way public bodies and members of the public view the relationship between one another.

CHAPTER 3

THE FREEDOM OF INFORMATION ACT 1997: PHILOSOPHY, IMPLEMENTATION AND IMPACT

Gerry Kearney*

The Freedom of Information Act passed into law on 21 April 1997. It followed from a commitment in the Government of Renewal programme to enact freedom of information legislation modelled on best practice abroad.

The context of the Act is one of remarkable reform and one which features a range of parallel reform measures including:

• Ethics in Public Office Act 1995;

• Electoral Act 1997;

• Public Service Management Act 1997;

• Compellability, Privileges and Immunities of Witnesses Act 1997;

• Cabinet Confidentiality referendum.

These initiatives are taking place in the context of the 'Delivering Better Government' initiative. It is important therefore to view the FOI Act as linked with a programme of wide ranging legislative, constitutional and administrative reforms.

PHILOSOPHY OF FOI

The long title sets out the purpose of the Freedom of Information Act. It asserts that the public is entitled to obtain access to official information to the greatest extent possible consistent with the public interest and the right to privacy.

---

*Gerry Kearney heads the Freedom of Information Central Policy Unit of the Department of Finance, which is currently overseeing arrangements for the implementation of the Freedom of Information Act.

The philosophy underlying freedom of information is broadly based on the following principles:

- When government is more open to public scrutiny it becomes more accountable.

- If people are adequately informed and have access to information, there is likely to be greater appreciation of issues involved in policy decisions and stronger public ownership and acceptance of decisions made.

- Groups and individuals who are affected by government decisions should know the criteria applied in making those decisions.

Every individual has a right:

(a) to know what information is held in government records about him or her personally, subject to certain exemptions to protect essential public interests;

(b) to inspect files held about or relating to him or her;

(c) to have inaccurate material on file corrected.

MAIN FEATURES OF THE ACT

The Act establishes three new statutory rights:

- a legal right for each person to access information held by public bodies;

- a legal right for each person to have official information relating to him or herself amended where it is incomplete, incorrect or misleading;

- a legal right to reasons for decisions affecting oneself.

These rights will be overseen by an independent Information Commissioner who will review decisions made by public bodies under the Act. Certain exemptions are proposed so as to protect key sensitive information of Government and of public bodies. These exemptions are based on standard practice in other countries with freedom of information legislation. Most of these exemptions are not absolute and many are subject to an overall test of whether disclosure would be in the public interest.

RELATIONSHIP WITH THE OFFICIAL SECRETS ACT

The Official Secrets Act 1963 prohibits the release of any official information unless duly authorised. By thus making all official information virtually secret, the OSA fails to distinguish between trivial, routine and extremely sensitive information. The FOI Act replaces this presumption of secrecy with a presumption of openness. In an appeal to the independent Information Commissioner, the onus is clearly on the public body to demonstrate that the refusal to disclose information in any particular case is justified. The Act also provides for the amendment of the Official Secrets Act so that where information is released under Freedom of Information, or in good faith that its release was so authorised, such release would not contravene that Act.

HOW DOES IT WORK?

Commencement   The Act will commence for all government departments and central offices twelve months from enactment, i.e. 21 April 1998. Local Authorities and Health Boards will come within its scope after a further six months. The Minister for Finance may, by regulations, apply the Act to other bodies in the public sector, those funded by Government and those carrying out statutory duties.

Procedures Governing Access   The right of access will be exercised by a person asking directly for the information from the public body concerned. Public bodies will normally have up to four weeks in which to respond to a request. The Act imposes an obligation on public bodies to assist the public when making requests for such information. Where a request is refused, reasons for the refusal and the grounds on which it is based, must normally be given.

Publication of Material by Public Bodies   To assist the public to focus their requests for information, public bodies are required to publish information on their structure, functions and categories of information they hold. In addition public bodies must publish the internal rules, guidelines, precedents, etc. used by them in making decisions.

Delegation   Functions of heads of public bodies may be delegated to other officers in the organisation. This enables decisions on the release of information to be taken at lower levels in a public body. It also allows the operation of an effective internal review system.

Charges   Fees may be charged in respect of the retrieval and copying of records, based on a standard hourly rate, to be prescribed by the Minister of Finance. No charges will apply in relation to the location of records containing personal information, save where a large number of records are involved.

WHAT INFORMATION MAY BE ACCESSED?

The following records will be available under the FOI Act from commencement:

- all records created from commencement date;

- all personal records irrespective of when created;

- any other records necessary to the understanding of a current record;

- all personnel records, created less than three years before commencement, of staff in public bodies. Earlier records may be accessed if they are liable to be used in a way that might adversely affect the interests of the member of staff involved.

The Minister for Finance may extend the scope of the Act, by regulations, to include earlier records, or records relating to a particular subject matter created prior to commencement.

EXEMPT RECORDS

Part III of the Act sets out a series of related measures to protect information concerning key areas of government activity. Many of the protections outlined can be set aside where the public interest would, on balance, be better served by the disclosure than by the withholding of the records in question.
    The exemptions fall into the following broad areas:

- deliberations of government and of public bodies;

- operations of public bodies;

- law enforcement, public safety;

- defence, security and international relations;

- information obtained in confidence;

- commercially sensitive information;

- personal information;

- financial and economic interests of the State;

- legal, parliamentary and court matters;

- research and natural resources.

Key features of the approach adopted in the FOI Act, in relation to exemptions are as follows:

- *an injury test.* In many cases information may be withheld only if it can be demonstrated that a specific harm or injury would arise from disclosure. The fact that a document falls within a particular category of information is not, in itself, sufficient reason for its withholding;

- *a public interest test.* Most of the exemptions are not absolute but are subject to an overall test of whether disclosure would be in the public interest;

- *consultation procedures in relation to third party records.* The Act upholds the privacy of persons who have given information of a personal, commercially sensitive or confidential nature. Such information may not be disclosed in the public interest without first consulting the person concerned and allowing him or her an opportunity to appeal the decision.

REVIEW AND APPEAL PROCEDURES

The Act provides for internal review against an initial decision by a public body. Such a review must be undertaken at a higher level than that at which the original decision was made and be completed within three weeks. Overseas experience suggests that 30 to 40 per cent of appeals may be resolved in this way.

An independent Office of Information Commissioner is established under the Act to review decisions under the Act. The Commissioner has wide powers to summon witnesses and examine documents. His or her decisions will be binding on the parties concerned, subject only to appeal to the High Court on a point of law. In addition the Commissioner is required to keep the operation of the Act under review and may carry out investigations into procedures adopted by public bodies for the purpose of compliance with its provisions.

BENEFITS OF FOI

Robert Hazell conducted a study of the effects of FOI in Australia, New Zealand and Canada as part of a UK Civil Service Travelling Fellowship.[1] Having reviewed the operation of the legislation in all three jurisdictions, he identified the benefits of FOI as including the following:

- individual access to one's own personal information has been the great success story of FOI;

- better understanding between public bodies and their clients;

---

1. Hazell "Freedom of Information in Australia, Canada and New Zealand" *Public Administration* 67(2) (1989) pp.189-210.

- the publication of internal rules and guidelines has increased public awareness of the decision-making process;

- improvement in the quality of primary decision making;

- improvement in the standard of report writing with information being more factual, more accurate and more carefully thought out;

- greater openness in departments' personnel practices.

Concerns were widely expressed abroad when FOI was being introduced in the early 1980s in Canada, Australia and New Zealand as to its adverse effects on public administration. It was feared that it would fundamentally change the way in which government business was conducted, and that the frankness and candour of advice from officials would suffer. These deeply held views were publicly aired by leading politicians and public servants to parliamentary committee hearings.

Robert Hazell concluded, from speaking to senior civil servants, that it was impossible to find any evidence to substantiate these fears. Subsequent reviews of the impact of the legislation in both Canada and Australia also found that the operation of FOI had delivered significant benefits in their respective jurisdictions.

This view is supported by the Attorney General's Department in Canberra, Australia which has advised "that FOI has not had a detrimental effect on frankness and candour amongst public servants, and on the contrary, has improved the quality of advice and recorded information".[2]

Similarly, the President of the Privy Council, Canada indicated that one of the principal effects of FOI has been to improve the drafting of documents because of the possibility of publication. He went on to state that he had not yet seen evidence to support the view that the Access Act is causing a fundamental change in the conduct of officials or ministers.[3]

PREPARATIONS FOR FOI UNDERWAY IN PUBLIC BODIES

Change takes time and effort. Experience elsewhere has demonstrated that effective preparation by public bodies in advance of commencement date is the key to successful implementation of the Freedom of Information Act.

Recognising the importance of adequate preparations the FOI Act provided for one year's lead-in prior to commencement. It is appropriate therefore to say a few words about the mechanisms and tasks involved in preparations undertaken for the Act.

---

2. Personal communication.
3. See Hazell, *op. cit.*

Preparations have been approached at three levels:

(a) an Interdepartmental Working Group;

(b) an FOI Central Policy Unit within the Department of Finance;

(c) internal FOI groups within each department to oversee implementation locally.

The FOI Interdepartmental Working Group has served to identify common issues to be addressed, to develop options and perspectives and to approve strategies of best practice. This Group has served to broaden ownership and cross-departmental involvement in the implementation process, as well as focusing the efforts of departments in a coherent and purposeful way. The Group's membership comprises representatives from all Departments/Offices and a number of other public bodies which come within the scope of the Act from commencement.

To support the work of the cross-departmental group and of departments, an FOI *Central Policy Unit* has been established in the Department of Finance. This undertakes a number of key functions.

• It chairs and directs the work of the main group.

• It co-ordinates and disseminates legal advice.

• It develops and, where appropriate, delivers FOI training.

• It provides practical guidance on organisational arrangements necessary.

• It formulates strategies for tackling issues of common interest to departments.

Complementing these arrangements an internal working group has been established in each department chaired at Assistant Secretary level. At present these serve to oversee implementation locally. In particular these internal groups ensure that information and training on FOI is provided to all grades in their respective departments. After commencement it is envisaged that these groups will constitute local experts who will provide key advice and departmental ownership of FOI.

The key tasks involved in preparing for FOI fall into three broad areas:

• training;

• publications;

• record management

Training. An unprecedented programme of training has been underway for FOI since September 1997. As of May 1998 close on 3,000 civil servants have received centrally provided FOI training. The nature of the training will vary having regard to the needs of three broad groups within departments and public bodies:

- overview training is being provided for staff generally;
- specialised training is being provided for those who will be decision-makers under the Act;
- advanced training is being provided for key personnel who will constitute local experts in each department.

I should say that the training of 3,000 is just the start. There will be an ongoing programme of FOI training so as to ensure that departmental personnel are fully skilled in FOI and remain so. This work is being complemented by "in-house" training which many departments are providing directly to their staff; greater numbers will have received training within their own departments and offices.

Publications. I mentioned earlier that, to assist the public in exercising their rights of access, the Act requires the production of certain publications by government bodies. The purpose of these publications is to set out the general structure of each organisation, the services it delivers, rights of appeal, types of records held and arrangements in place to facilitate access to these under FOI. In addition each public body must set out the internal rules, guidelines, practices and precedents it uses for the purposes of decision making. In this way the public will be fully informed as to the way in which decisions are made, rights of appeal and what information is held by each public body. It is intended that these publications will be available from each department by 21 April 1998.

Record Management. The advent of technology has led to a significant disimprovement in record management practices in government bodies in recent years. Staffing restrictions, coupled with the advance of IT have led to a decline in good record management. Many files are no longer held, or even recorded, in a central registry. Instead, a folder culture has developed, under which individual sections frequently create and hold their own papers. This can lead to an absence of comprehensive departmental knowledge or control of its own records.

Given that a central tenet of the FOI Act is the provision of responses to requests for information within specified time limits, it is vital that decision makers in public bodies have instant access to records being sought. Arising from the requirements of the FOI Act, departments and offices have been overhauling and modernising their record keeping systems.

"FOI – NOT EXACTLY THE ANSWER TO A REPORTERS' PRAYERS"

I thought I might conclude by referring to an interesting paper by Jack Water-ford, a leading Australian journalist, on FOI, or more accurately, the relation-ship between journalists and the legislation.[4]

In his paper, Waterford makes a number of quite critical comments in relation to the reluctance of many journalists to meet the challenges posed by FOI. He refers to many journalists describing FOI as Freedom *from* Informa-tion.

In particular he points to:

(a) a frequent lack of familiarity by journalists with the processes of deci-sion-making in government;

(b) a consequential difficulty in identifying the routine from the irregular.

Waterford suggests that to make FOI useful for themselves, journalists need to learn and understand public administration so as to know what is routine, how decisions are made, and who would be involved. Only by achieving such mastery, he argues, can a journalist identify and investigate irregularities in practice or decision making. Clearly, the challenges referred to by Jack Wa-terford are no less relevant for journalists here.

CONCLUSION

The single message from jurisdictions abroad is that the people who enjoy and avail most frequently of FOI are the ordinary members of the public. Approximately 90 per cent of FOI requests are from this group. It is with and through members of the public that FOI helps to deepen democracy and en-hance citizens' rights.

---

4. Paper to a Meeting of the Records Managers' Association, unpublished.

CHAPTER 4

FREEDOM OF INFORMATION: THE NEXT STEPS

Eithne Fitzgerald[*]

INTRODUCTION

The Official Secrets Act has symbolised a culture of secrecy which permeated Irish political and administrative practice since independence. The first thing I had to do on entering the civil service at nineteen was to sign the Official Secrets Act. There is a comfort factor in living with the certainties of official secrecy and, in designing the Freedom of Information Act, a great deal of attention was paid to how access to information could become a reality in a public service long used to doing its business in another way. Over-turning a culture of secrecy requires more than just legislation – it requires leadership, training, administrative systems, which facilitate the retrieval of information, active promotion of the right to information and an appeals system which copperfastens the citizen's right to information.

HISTORY

The first Freedom of Information Bill was tabled in the Senate by Senator Brendan Ryan to little official enthusiasm. Organisations such as 'Let in the Light' and the NUJ have long campaigned for a Freedom of Information Act as a central part of a broader campaign on freedom of expression. Effectively, however, the movement towards FOI only became part of the mainstream political agenda with the commitment in the Fianna Fáil/Labour programme for government of 1993 "to consider a Freedom of Information Act". This task, along with a wider programme of reform under the heading "Broadening our Democracy" was assigned to the Office of the Tánaiste.

Labour in 1992 had unsuccessfully sought a firmer commitment to legis-

---

***Eithne Fitzgerald** was the Minister of State at the Office of the Tánaiste from 1993 to 1997. She prepared and steered through the Freedom of Information Act.

late, but political events during 1994 served to strengthen the political climate for change and lent weight to the work underway on preparing outline proposals for legislation. In the aftermath of the Beef Tribunal Report with its spotlight on economy of official information, Taoiseach Albert Reynolds gave a formal commitment in the Dáil to legislate for freedom of information. 'Openness, transparency and accountability' became a political mantra following the downfall of the Reynolds' Government in November 1994, and the subsequent government programme, a 'Government of Renewal', contained an explicit commitment to legislate and a timetable.

The Heads of the Bill were published in December 1995, and debated in Dáil committee over the following two months. In the meantime, Senator Dick Roche had tabled his own Freedom of Information Bill, closely based on the Norwegian legislation, a clear indication that all-party support was now secured. The final Government Bill was published in December 1996 and enacted April in 1997. The Seanad debate in particular was very constructive and informed, and contributions from Dick Roche, Joe Lee, Jan O'Sullivan and others led to some important improvements in the draft Bill as it stood.

In coming late in the day to enacting legislation in this area, we had a great number of models of legislation and of practical experience on which to draw. The experience in practice with the Access to Information on the Environment Regulations enacted two years previously offered a lot of cautionary lessons on what to avoid if access to information was to become a reality for citizens and to be practical for public bodies.

STRONG INDEPENDENT APPEALS SYSTEM

It became clear that a strong, effective and independent appeals system would be critical in ensuring that access to information would really work. While less of an issue for a society such as Sweden with laws and a tradition of openness stretching back 230 years, a strong appeals system is essential in establishing the public's right to know in a political and administrative system steeped in the culture of secrecy.

Weaknesses in the Canadian appeals mechanism have hampered the effectiveness of their legislation. An appeal system modelled on the Australian Administrative Appeals Tribunal would be an excessively formal mechanism in my view, likely to give rise to excess delays. I opted instead for an office of Information Commissioner. I am delighted that Kevin Murphy, the Ombudsman, agreed to be Ireland's first Information Commissioner.

The appeals system provides, in the first instance, for internal review by a more senior officer within an organisation of an initial decision to refuse disclosure. Experience abroad suggests that 30 to 40 per cent of cases can be settled at this level. If a decision to refuse goes on appeal to the Information Commissioner the onus of proof lies on the public body to show why the information should not be released, and how the balancing tests – a 'harm test' or a 'public interest test' – have been applied.

THE BALANCE OF PUBLIC INTEREST

A key feature of the Act is that, where there is a judgement call to be made, the authorities or on appeal the Information Commissioner, must consider whether the public interest would be better served by disclosing rather than withholding information. The mandate, set out in the Long Title of the Act, effectively its purpose clause, is "to enable members of the public to obtain access, to the greatest extent possible consistent with the public interest and the right to privacy, to information in the possession of public bodies...".

The exemptions are generally discretionary, not mandatory, and require that the option to exempt information from disclosure must be weighed against how, on balance, the public interest is best served. In the case of material relating to defence, security, international relations or the justice system, the key criterion is whether release of the information would give rise to harm, not the subject matter of the request itself. The strong thrust of the Act is therefore to favour openness.

WHAT THE ACT WILL MEAN FOR CITIZENS?

The commencement from 21 April 1998 of the Freedom of Information Act marked an important start, where the public have a legal right to information from central government departments and 49 public bodies under their aegis. Six months later, on 21 October 1998, Health Boards and Local Authorities came under the Act.

People now have a legal right to see public files and public documents. This is a very important balance on the operation of the political and administrative systems because any file can be sought and access will normally be granted. This puts out in the open the information behind policy, the deliberative processes of public bodies and the options and how they were weighed before any change in policy.

This right will be of particular value to community groups and to campaigning organisations.

Experience abroad suggests that the requirement to do business in the open has improved the quality of public administration and of decision making. The likelihood of open public scrutiny generally results in better standards of policy evaluation and of record keeping.

Personal information

In particular, people have a legal right to see personal information about themselves on public file, which will give them full access to files on their own case – their own tax files, welfare files, grant applications, medical files (in a Health Board hospital) and social work files.

People have dealings with public bodies every day of their lives, as taxpayers, welfare recipients, parents of school children, as people in business, as workers with rights. Information is power and freedom of information will transfer power from those who work behind closed doors to ordinary citizens.

People can also seek amendment or deletion of personal information which is inaccurate or misleading.

Reasons for decisions

Public bodies are required to publish their internal rules, guidelines and circulars, which will greatly enhance the individual's right to fair procedure in dealings with any public body. It also poses a discipline on public bodies to examine their guidelines for the exercise of discretionary powers to ensure they are fair and consistent. This provision requires the publication of the guidelines used by, for example, community welfare officers.

The Act also requires public bodies to give reasons for their decisions, giving the findings on matters of fact, and relating these findings, to the rules of the particular scheme.

Taken together, these provisions on personal files, on publication of internal rules and on reasons for decisions, amount to a powerful charter of citizens' rights in relation to the individual's dealings with the State.

Politics in the open

Opening up the books and files will strengthen the accountability of politicians and the public service. By giving everyone access to the information, which underlies policy choices, it can facilitate more informed public debate about policy options. Bringing the analysis of policy options into the open is the best guarantee that that analysis will be thorough and will examine a range of alternative policy choices. The information deficit of an opposition compared to a government can be largely redressed if those in opposition make effective use of FOI. For example, obscure replies to Parliamentary Questions will become irrelevant if the deputy tabling the question has access to the file containing further information and material for replies to possible supplementaries, not to mention access to the primary file on the subject.

The media will play an important role in sifting the vast amount of material to become available under FOI and how accountable the system becomes in practice will be strongly linked to how effectively they do their job. 'Journalism by leak' may become less important when key information is legally available, and the skills of analysing large quantities of material for their significance may become of more importance. Asking the right questions will still be a key skill, when confronted with a potential glut of information.

A culture of openness

Building a culture of openness will take intensive training for public servants, some inevitable settling in time, and a period where the work of the Information Commissioner spells out how the tests in the Act are interpreted in practice. Experience in other countries suggests that after an initial period, the system adapts to the new climate, and living with openness becomes as much the norm as living with official secrecy had been for generations.

A genuinely open and active information policy will not just sit back and wait for requests for information to come in, but look actively at how people can be offered information. For example, a request for information on one type of welfare benefit should be able to trigger the offer of information on other relevant benefits for those in that position.

An active information programme will look not only at the supply of information, but how information is best transmitted to, and received by, those who need to know more. It will move beyond the technology of the leaflet to explore the best media to get a message to particular audiences. The potential for transfer of information through modern IT is enormous and has barely been explored in terms of the interaction of citizens and the State. With 80 per cent of homes without a personal computer, there would seem to be a lot of merit in developing community access points through the public library service and the Community Information Centres, under the auspices of the National Social Service Board.

THE NEXT STEPS

The enactment of the Freedom of Information Act does not mark the end of the political tasks. The Act provides for the designation by regulation of other public bodies to whom the Act will apply. This includes bodies, such as the Gardaí, semi-State bodies, voluntary organisations, which are wholly or partly publicly funded such as voluntary secondary schools, voluntary hospitals and major players in the health field like St Michael's House and Rehab.

The Act provides for immediate access to full personal records and access to current files. The intention is to ensure that public bodies will in the first instance put in place an information retrieval system for current and future records, which would facilitate public access, as international experience indicates that the general public's main interest will be in current records.

The Act provides, however, that by regulation the time period can be rolled back either for groups of records or for all records, so that ultimately

Freedom of Information can meet up with the Archives Act.

The purpose of the phased introduction was clearly outlined to the Oireachtas – to ensure that administrative systems would be in place from day one to allow for the smooth operation of the Act and to ensure its effective operation from the outset.

When the operation of the Act has settled down after this initial period, the phasing in of access to back records should begin. The Act also explicitly provides that it is not intended to bar access to information, other than by way of the Act, and there is a role for the Information Commissioner in encouraging the active release of information, whether under the Act or otherwise.

The Act provides exemption for matters covered by secrecy clauses in other enactments, but puts in place a procedure for systematic review of these by an Oireachtas committee and for independent advice from the Information Commissioner as to whether such clauses should be retained, modified or entirely repealed.

OFFICIAL SECRETS ACT

The Freedom of Information Act effectively turns the Official Secrets Act on its head, replacing the presumption of official secrecy with the presumption of a right to know. It expressly lifts the operation of section 4 of the OSA for information coming under the Freedom of Information Act. Effectively the main remaining effect of the Official Secrets Act is a regime of criminal penalties for unauthorised disclosure of such information as remains exempt from access.

The Dáil Committee on Legislation and Security has completed a review of the OSA. It has recommended its total repeal, and replacement with a measure which would distinguish between serious improper disclosure of information, which would continue to attract serious sanction, and minor improper disclosure which would be dealt with at a disciplinary level.

Protecting Whistle-blowers

Some detailed work has been undertaken in relation to awarding legal protection against disciplinary action or dismissal for people who 'blow the whistle' on serious wrong-doing which they encounter in the course of their work. This work was not complete in time to include it in the Freedom of Information Act. Given the almost accidental nature of the disclosures at the heart of the political system in relation to Haughey and Lowry, and the continuing secrecy in relation to the Ansbacher accounts, it is clear that there is need for a suitable mechanism which can allow people to come forward without fear to disclose their suspicions of wrongdoing, be that in the public or the private sector.

This needs careful design to ensure that it provides a suitable mechanism which can allow proper investigation of alleged wrong-doing while preventing nuisance complaints against colleagues from de-railing legitimate disciplinary action.

A PRIVACY ACT

The death of Diana, Princess of Wales has led to renewed calls for privacy legislation to curb press excesses. The Law Reform Commission has published a discussion document on privacy and the National Newspapers of Ireland have published what in my view is a very inadequate privacy code – a code which would for example regard the children of public figures as "legitimate targets". In an increasingly cut-throat media world where people's legitimate right to privacy has increasingly been sacrificed in battles for circulation, I feel it is now appropriate to address this issue through legislation.

DATA PROTECTION

Personal information held on computer is subject to protection, and the extension of similar protection to personal information held in manual records is coming down the road from the EU. An important benefit would be to give people a legal right to see their own medical records whether or not they have been treated in a publicly funded system.

ADMINISTRATIVE PROCEDURES BILL

Preliminary work has been undertaken on an Administrative Procedures Bill which would set out standards of service and response times which customers of public services can expect. Work on a new Ombudsman Bill is more advanced which would extend the remit of the Ombudsman to include bodies receiving substantial public funding, and would make his decisions legally binding. These pieces of legislation would provide important further enhancement of the consumer rights already incorporated in the Freedom of Information Act.

CONCLUSION

Freedom of information has the potential to build a new relationship between citizens and the State, between the public and those who serve them. It offers a radical transformation of the culture of secrecy under which our State has operated for three quarters of a century. The Act provides a strong framework, but there is still work to be done in ensuring that framework is used to the full, and I look forward to completion of the legislative tasks which still remain.

CHAPTER 5

The Freedom of Information Act 1997: A Comparative Perspective

Maeve McDonagh[*]

Freedom of information legislation is a feature of most modern Western democracies, with our nearest neighbour being one notable exception. Overseas FOI legislation was one of the most important forces which influenced the shape of the Irish FOI Act. The aim of this paper is to evaluate some of the main features of the Irish Act by comparing them with their overseas counterparts. The following features of the legislation will be explored briefly: the exemptions, the scope of the Act, the method of enforcement. The comparisons will focus mainly on those common law countries which operate under a Westminster style of government, namely Australia, Canada and New Zealand.

Such an evaluation will help to assess the potential impact of the rights conferred by the Freedom of Information Act 1997. There are of course a number of other factors which will determine the practical impact of the Act. These include domestic legal imperatives such as the constitutional backdrop to the operation of the Act as well as cultural factors. Even more important will be the approach of the Information Commissioner to his task of enforcing the Act. As we will see, the Irish FOI Act relies heavily on the judgement of the Information Commissioner who is the person charged with enforcing the Act. The approach of the first Irish Information Commissioner will, therefore, be a key factor in determining the success of this Act.

FOI IN THE COMMON LAW WORLD

The introduction of FOI legislation in the common law world began in 1966

***Maeve McDonagh** is a lecturer in the Law Faculty, NUI, Cork. She is the author of many publications on freedom of information, including, *Freedom of Information Law in Ireland* (Round Hall Sweet and Maxwell, 1998).

in the US. It was followed by Australia and New Zealand in 1982 and Canada in 1983. FOI legislation has also been widely introduced at state and provincial level in the US, Canada and Australia.

THE EXEMPTIONS

All of the legislation contains roughly the same list of exemption provisions. These include cabinet records, records which would reveal the deliberative processes of public bodies, law enforcement records, records relating to personal information of third parties, records containing commercially sensitive information, information given in confidence, etc. There are however, differences in the manner of their formulation.

The drafting of the exemptions in the Irish Act has been influenced more by the Australian and Canadian Acts than by the US or New Zealand legislation. The exemptions in the Canadian and Australian Acts, like those in the Irish Act, are detailed and specific. The New Zealand and US Acts, on the other hand, adopt an open text approach in that exemptions are stated in fairly terse terms leaving it to those enforcing the legislation to flesh them out. The former approach has the advantage of spelling out the circumstances in which the exemption will apply, thus making the manner of operation of the Act easier for users and public bodies to predict and also making it easier for those enforcing the Act to determine the legislators' intentions. On the other hand, it can lead to very complex formulations. In the Seanad debate on the Bill, Senator Joe Lee referred to the text as "reaching the outer limits of obscurity".

In terms of their contents, the Irish exemptions are drafted in a manner which is at least as broad as their overseas counterparts. The law enforcement exemption, in particular, is probably more detailed and extensive than any of its overseas equivalents. It is not surprising that there was such a 'belt and braces' approach to the protection of law enforcement information, given the reported opposition of the Department of Justice to the application of the freedom of information legislation to its records.

On the other hand, evidence of independent thinking is to be found in the Irish Act in features such as the exception to the deliberative processes exemption for reports on the performance of public bodies. This exception has no counterpart in overseas legislation. It will ensure that public bodies cannot refuse to disclose reports concerning their performance, on the basis that they relate to the bodies' decision-making processes. Thus, for example, a review of the operations of the Blood Transfusion Services Board could not be withheld on the grounds that it contains information relating to the deliberative processes of the Board.

An important feature of the exemptions in the Irish FOI Act is the heavy reliance on public interest tests. Generally speaking such tests allow for the

disclosure of records which come within the terms of an exemption, in circumstances where the public interest would be better served by granting, than
by refusing the request for access. Public interest tests are a feature of just
over half of the exemption provisions. This constitutes a more extensive reliance on such tests than is found in the FOI Acts of the other common law
jurisdictions and contrasts with Canada in particular, where there is no provision for public interest tests. The inclusion of these tests may serve to mitigate
the effects of the relatively broad approach to the framing of the exemptions.
The approach of the Information Commissioner to the application of the public interest tests will be crucial in this regard.

SCOPE

The Act applies only to those bodies which are listed in its First Schedule.
The Canadian and New Zealand Acts have the same approach to defining the
scope of their legislation as we do. The advantage of this approach is that it
makes it easy to ascertain whether or not the Act applies to a particular entity.
On the other hand, it requires constant updating as new bodies are created.
The Australian Act, on the other hand, applies to all public bodies except for
those listed in the Act. The advantage of the Australian approach is that its
scope is potentially much broader and it does not require amendment of the
Act to cater for newly created bodies.

The First Schedule to the Irish Act includes all the Departments of State
as well as 50 agencies of Central Government. These include: the Office of
the Attorney General, the Office of the Director of Public Prosecutions, the
Revenue Commissioners, the Social Welfare Appeals Office, the Office of
the Ombudsman and the Office of the Comptroller and Auditor General. The
Environmental Protection Agency and An Bord Pleanála were late inclusions
to the First Schedule, having been added at Report stage in the Dáil.

There is provision for the automatic extension of the Act to Health Boards
and Local Authorities within six months of commencement of the Act. The
scope of the Act can also be extended to other bodies by regulation. Such
extensions can, however, only take place with the consent of the Minister
responsible for that body. The bodies to which the application of the Act can
be thus extended are also listed in the Act. They include: the Garda Síochána,
bodies established under statute, bodies financed from the public purse, companies a majority of the shares of which are held by a Minister, bodies appointed by the Government or a Minister, bodies on which functions have
been conferred in respect of the general public, and a subsidiary of any of the
aforementioned bodies.[1]

We can compare the scope of the Irish Act with its overseas counterparts.

---

1. Paragraph 1(5), First Schedule.

In Australia, where the Act covers all agencies apart from those expressly excluded, the scope of the Act extends to all significant public sector bodies with only about 20 agencies being expressly excluded. The list of bodies covered by the Canadian and New Zealand legislation is extensive. In New Zealand for example, the Act applies to approximately 200 public bodies apart from government departments. Its scope extends to universities, schools, hospitals, the national broadcasting company, the national airline and various semi-State bodies. In Canada, the Act covers over 100 government bodies apart from government departments and its scope extends to a number of semi-State organisations.

Comparatively speaking then, the scope of the Irish Act is somewhat limited. Unlike its overseas counterparts it does not cover the police force. Nor does it extend to schools or universities or to voluntary hospitals or to government agencies such as Bord Fáilte, Forbairt, FÁS, the Health and Safety Executive and commercial State-sponsored bodies such as Aer Lingus, the ESB, Coillte, Bord Gáis and RTÉ.

There is, however, scope for all of these bodies to be brought within the reach of the Act through the introduction of the necessary regulations. Indeed, there is scope for the application of the Irish Act beyond the public sector in that it can be extended to bodies on which functions have been conferred in respect of the public. This could include bodies such as The Law Society. Cynics might feel however that once there is a Freedom of Information Act in place it is unlikely that its scope will be extended.

METHOD OF ENFORCEMENT

Different approaches have been adopted in various jurisdictions to the enforcement of freedom of information laws. Most jurisdictions provide opportunities for both internal and external review of decisions. A system of internal review is useful in terms of offering a speedy and inexpensive method of resolving disputes. Other perceived advantages of internal review are that it reduces the number of complaints going to external review and improves the management culture of public agencies. However, in order to establish the impartiality of the review process, the institution of an external review system is essential. Three main models of external review have emerged in freedom of information legislation in the common law world.

The first relies on the courts to enforce the law. This is the method of review relied upon in the US and (as a second tier of review) in Canada. Review of FOI decisions by the courts is – mainly for reasons of expense, delay and formality – not a desirable option. Another problem is that the courts are, by nature, generalist bodies and do not have detailed knowledge of specialised areas of law like freedom of information law. Nor is there any possibility of a court adopting an overall supervisory role in enforcing legislation;

rather it is confined to reacting to individual cases as they arise.

Another model uses a tribunal to review decisions. In Australia, for example, primary responsibility for disposing of federal FOI appeals lies in the hands of the Administrative Appeals Tribunal. Tribunals have a number of advantages over courts in terms of reviewing FOI decisions. They are generally fast, inexpensive and relatively informal. They are also in a position to engage in a greater degree of specialisation than the courts. Where reliance is placed on tribunals as the sole agent of external review however, there is an absence of overall monitoring of the operation of the legislation.

The third model involves the carrying out of FOI reviews by an Ombudsman or Information Commissioner. Generally speaking an Ombudsman will take on his or her FOI jurisdiction as an adjunct to his or her main function of resolving disputes concerning maladministration in the public sector generally. An Information Commissioner is usually someone who has been appointed specifically to deal with Freedom of Information disputes. Another distinction which can often be made between an Ombudsman and Information Commissioner is that decisions of Ombudsmen are usually in the form of non-binding recommendations whereas Information Commissioners may or may not be binding.

In Canada, the first level of review is in the hands of a specialist Information Commissioner who does not have the power to make legally binding decisions. In New Zealand, the office of Ombudsman, which had originally been established to deal with complaints of maladministration against public sector bodies, was given the responsibility of reviewing FOI decisions following the passing of the FOI legislation. The New Zealand Ombudsman is, in theory, restricted to recommending disclosure of information. However, such recommendations become binding if they are not vetoed within 20 days. In some of the Australian and Canadian state and provincial statutes, specialist Information Commissioners with power to make binding decisions on access have been provided for.[2] The strength of the specialist Ombudsman/Information Commissioner model lies in the fact that unlike a general purpose Ombudsman or the courts, he or she is dealing with only one area of law, thus making it possible for the holder of the office to become expert on the detail of the legislation and more importantly on the aims and objectives of the legislation. The Ombudsman/Information Commissioner can also take on the important task of monitoring the operation and effectiveness of the legislation overall to see, for example, whether it is having the desired impact on the day-to-day operations of public bodies. Such a task would be beyond the scope of the courts or a tribunal. However a weakness of the Ombudsman/Information Commissioner model can be that his or her decisions are sometimes not legally

2. *Canada*: Quebec, Ontario, British Colombia, Alberta; *Australia*: Queensland, Western Australia.

enforceable. Courts and tribunals, on the other hand, make decisions which are legally enforceable. Even where the Ombudsman/Information Commissioner's decisions are legally binding, problems can arise in terms of approach, in particular where the same individual is exercising the enforceable FOI jurisdiction along with a general purpose Ombudsman's jurisdiction. Attention was drawn by one commentator in the following terms to the differences between the traditional role of the Ombudsman and that of an Ombudsman/Information Commissioner exercising a FOI jurisdiction:

> Freedom of information disputes are always disputes over law: every case raises issues of statutory interpretation and application. They are a different diet from the traditional 'maladministration' fare of the office which is capable of resolution in almost every case by thorough investigation, discussion, persuasion and often, negotiation and compromise.[3]

The system of review adopted under the Freedom of Information Act 1997 is one which involves the use of internal review followed by the hearing of appeals by an Information Commissioner. The Irish Information Commissioner has the power to issue legally binding decisions. The Information Commissioner is also vested with powers to monitor the operation of the FOI Act. The Act allows for the appointment of the Ombudsman as Information Commissioner. The first holder of the office of Information Commissioner is the Ombudsman, Mr Kevin Murphy.

The adoption of the Information Commissioner model is in keeping with modern developments in FOI legislation overseas. It would, however, have been preferable, given the different styles of implementation required in respect of FOI and general Ombudsman legislation, had the offices of Information Commissioner and Ombudsman remained separate from one another. The essentially legal character of FOI disputes must be acknowledged. One important factor in determining the success of the Information Commissioner model in Ireland will be the extent to which his decisions will be fully explained and made available to the public. The Acts gives the Commissioner the power to publish reports of reviews carried out by him or her.[4] There is no duty to make such reports available to the public but it is submitted that it would be going against the spirit of the Act for the Information Commissioner to fail to make his decisions available. The availability of those decisions will be crucial to the development of a coherent body of case law under the Act. The Commissioner may be willing to follow the example of overseas Information Commissioners such as those in New Zealand, Ontario and British Columbia and Queensland who have made the full text of their decisions available on the internet.

---

3. Eagles, Taggart & Liddell, *Freedom of Information in New Zealand* (Auckland, 1992) p. 546.
4. Section 34(10).

CONCLUSION

Comparatively speaking this is a good piece of legislation. It is probably the best that could be achieved at the time. Given recent events, such as the alleged leaking of confidential Foreign Affairs documents, I would surmise that it is better than anything that could be achieved at present. In terms of its shortcomings, it is clear that most urgent attention is required in relation to the scope of the Act. It remains to be seen whether the political will exists to extend the scope of this Act further. Apart from that, the success of the Act will depend to a great extent on the approach taken by the Information Commissioner to its implementation.

CHAPTER 6

NEW INFORMATION AND COMMUNICATION TECHNOLOGIES, CITIZENSHIP NEEDS AND EUROPE'S WAY INTO THE INFORMATION SOCIETY

Dr Paschal Preston*

SCOPE OF THE PAPER

In Europe, as elsewhere, much of the recent public discourse concerning new information technologies and innovative communication systems (such as the internet) has tended to focus upon their universal benefits. This is clearly the case with the suppliers' marketing materials but much of the mass media coverage also strongly favours the technology producers' conceptions of the design, technical characteristics and potential applications of the new technologies. It is generally asserted that the new information and communication technologies (ICTs) are very flexible and pervasive in their applications and have the potential to increase productivity in information processing and distribution in most if not all contexts. They are perceived to match neatly most information users' pressing information and communication needs. The users' efficiency and economic welfare is enhanced when they purchase, or otherwise gain access to, the new technologies and applications and adopt them to their own specific needs and requirements.

Similarly, in the recent discourses surrounding the information superhighway (ISH) and what the EC Commission has termed "Europe's Way to the Information Society"[1] we find parallel claims about the universal benefits

---

*Dr Paschal Preston** is senior lecturer in the School of Communications, Dublin City University.

1. "Europe's way to the Information Society: an action plan" communication from the Commission to the Council and the European Parliament and to the Economic and

and efficiencies of these innovative technologies and systems. In this case the claimed benefits and efficiencies are often more political and social in scope than purely economic. A frequently encountered claim is that new ICTs, and especially the new broadband/multimedia applications which are anticipated to run over the 'information superhighway', will dramatically improve citizens' relationship with government, particularly in the areas of information search and exchange.[2]

In addition, we also find that many contemporary discussions of the role and influence of 'users' in shaping information and communication technologies and their applications frequently tend to define users in terms of consumers. Indeed even in the area of public services, there has been a marked shift in terminology applied to users of such services over the past decade – from customers to consumers.

In the electronic communications and related industrial sectors, the dominant discourses tend to define three separate categories of consumers: large private and public sector corporations, small/medium-sized firms and final or household consumers. Quite often, however, these three categories of consumer are conflated with the result that important distinctions are often neglected in some EC policy documents dealing with electronic communication services.[3]

This paper, however, will focus on a fourth and much neglected category of users – citizens. Despite this neglect, I wish to indicate how the interests of this particular category of user are closely bound up with alternative approaches to the design and implementation of new information infrastructures and communication networks and associated policy debates.

Thus this paper focuses on the 'citizens' and specific aspects of their information use and needs as one particular category of potential users of new information and communication technologies and networks. It draws upon a recently completed multi-country study undertaken by the author in collaboration with researchers based in four other EU Member States. This study sought to examine the extent and features of need/demand for specific forms

Social Committee and the Committee of Regions. Brussels: CEC, 1994 COM(94) 347 final.
2. See "Growth, Competitiveness and Employment: The Challenges and Ways Forward into the 21st Century" (White Paper). Luxembourg: OOPEC, 1994; "Europe and the Global Information Society: Recommendations to the European Council" report by Members of the High-Level Group on the Information Society (Bangemann Report), Brussels: CEC, 1994; "Europe's Way to the Information Society: An Action Plan" communication from the Commission to the Council and the European Parliament and to the Economic and Social Committee and the Committee of Regions, Brussels: CEC, 1994. COM(94) 347 final; "From Vision to Action: Info-Society 2000" (Copenhagen: Ministry of Research and IT) 1995.
3. Preston, "Technology, Space and Cohesion: Ireland and 'Europe's Way to the Information Society'" 13 (1996) No. 2/3, pp. 123–140 in 'The European Information Society' special issue of *Telematics and Informatics*.

of citizenship information within EU countries and the trends of change in such citizenship information needs, including the implications of new technologies in matching or meeting these needs.

Drawing from this research, the paper illustrates how this category of users has been largely marginalised from many of the current debates and discourses concerning new ICTs and infrastructures as well as information policy more generally. Within the dominant discourses, the rhetoric at least tends to privilege the interests or needs of the 'user' (usually defined as consumer) in shaping new communication technologies, information infrastructures and their related applications and policies. But this research indicates that some important needs and interests of citizens are not adequately reflected in the framing of current technology strategies or other information policies within EU member countries.[4]

The paper draws selectively from this recently completed research project and examines citizens as one relatively neglected aspect of information policy although they comprise a very large category of users or potential users of new information technologies and 'services'.

THE FRAMING AND SHAPING OF THE RESEARCH PROJECT

This paper is based on a research project which sought to examine:

a) the key characteristics and extent of both current and future needs/demands for citizenship information in Ireland;

b) the institutional and technological systems in place or emerging/being developed to address these needs.

The Broader Socio-Economic and Policy Context

To date there has been relatively little by way of comparative research on information and citizenship within EU Member States. This is not only because of resource costs but it is also because of the difficulties raised by the very distinctive policies towards citizenship information provision associated with different national political traditions.

In recent years, many EU Member States as well as the European Commission have sought to launch major national inquiries and public debates related to the economic and socio-political implications of new ICTs and their applications. The potential of new ICTs to radically transform citizens' access to governmental information has been a frequent theme within many of the

---

4. Preston, "Information and Citizenship in a European context: competing conceptions and definitions" presentation at EU DG XIII conference on *Information and Citizenship* Luxembourg, October, 1995. Summary of multi-country research project; Steele (ed.) *Information for Citizenship in Europe* (London: Policy Studies Institute) 1997.

recent discourses surrounding 'information superhighways' and 'Europe's way to the information society'.

At the same time, some national governments and the European Commission have been promoting the sale and re-sale of government-generated information as part of a strategy to develop the 'tradable information services sector' as an important component of the European 'information economy'. This policy thrust is serving to deepen the commodification of government information and this in turn raises certain implications for the terms and conditions of citizens' access to government-related information. These trends link directly to the information supherhighway/national information infrastructure (ISH/NII) debates and the concerns about a growing threat of social exclusion or polarisation based on differential access to information and communication resources or capabilities.

Quite apart from these ICT/ISH-related developments, there has been a significant surge of public debate on certain questions and issues related to information and citizenship in some Member States (e.g. UK and Ireland) since around 1990. This has been sparked by a number of major political and economic crises and scandals where questions of citizens' rights to access to information (and excessive secrecy) with respect to political and economic information have featured prominently. For example, in recent years, there has been an active if sporadic public debate concerning the conception and definition of citizenship and civic culture in Ireland. This has been manifest in commitments to create more pluralist and inclusive definitions of citizenship and identity on the part of all the major political parties and many pressure groups.

The quality and flow of citizenship information related to the EU-level of decision making and the associated construction of new conceptions of citizenship and national identity in Member States was also identified as an increasingly important issue for this comparative research project. But, for reasons of resource and time constraints, the research team decided that this issue would not feature prominently in the study but was one which must be addressed in future work.

Thus information and citizenship issues have been very much to the forefront of the agenda of 'live' political debate in many EU Member States and there is a wide perception that they have been undergoing something of a fundamental 'sea change'.

The Origins and Initial Shaping of this Research Project

The origins and funding of this particular project were important in shaping its direction and focus. It should be noted that in many respects it was rather unusual in that it falls outside the usual 'response' mode associated with most EU-funded R&D programmes. Thus, in keeping with the demands for more reflexivity within the academic research process, it may be worthwhile to outline briefly some of the key moments of the project's shaping and framing processes here.

The origin of this comparative research project was stimulated by a common interest amongst research team members in the above-mentioned developments and their implications for information and citizenship issues. Essentially, the framing, design and funding of the study were achieved via two-way communications between members of the research network and representatives of one of the EC directorates. The EC agreed to furnish some funding for a cross-country study which would help develop a basic definition and measure of changing citizens' information needs and wants in EU Member States which might be useful for policy planning purposes.

There was general agreement amongst all participants that this kind of research project was required because certain contextual changes appeared to be giving rise to major shifts in the demand for, and provision of, citizenship information. The major changes of concern can be summarised as follows:

Information and Citizenship in the EU: major contextual changes

- growth of public interest and concern, and debates over information and citizenship issues in Europe (including access to information; privacy; civil liberties etc.);

- pressures from the political and economic elites towards a fundamental shift in the roles of the public and private information sectors;

- the implications of new information and communication technologies (ICT), e.g. implication of information superhighways and internet/worldwide web for information and citizenship issues;

- pressures to reduce government expenditures leading to major changes in the public-sector organisations involved in delivery of information to citizens;

- the growing role of EU-level citizenship and information issues.

Having agreed to the study in principle, the sponsoring agency suggested that the national reports should address the following:

a)   review the key features of 'what is going on' in each country in the information and citizenship area;

b)   identify the 'live' issues, actions and concerns in each country and review the key relevant policy documents and other literature;

c)   undertake interviews with a wide selection of the relevant organisations.

The sponsor requested that each country report should focus on issues related to the relationship between the government and private persons/citizens, map and describe the key relevant issues, debates and practical developments, present examples of interesting/innovative practices and advance some initial policy recommendations. In addition, the sponsor indicated that the country reports should also consider how citizenship information services and related needs may be provided and transformable via the use of new electronic communication media technologies and services.

Summary of other Methodological Issues

It was agreed at the initial project planning meeting, that the research reports should reflect the sponsor's request that the focus should fall on the information needs of the majority of 'ordinary' citizens. But it was agreed too that the research must also be mindful of the possibilities and risks of 'exclusion' of various groups of citizens and interests. It was noted that there are a number of grey areas where the boundaries of what is or what is not relevant to the report are somewhat blurred. Thus it was agreed that the reports may occasionally address more than 'pure' information services (e.g. broker and advocate services) and the role of relevant voluntary, charity and other independent agencies.

The final overall research design and methodology was discussed and negotiated between the five research teams and representatives of the sponsor. At this stage, there was considerable discussion concerning the terms of reference for the study including:

a) should the research focus on 'demand' or 'need' for citizenship information? It was agreed to place the focus on the latter category;

b) the considerable difficulties involved in arriving at measures of such needs;

c) the extent to which the study should include consideration of (individual/household) consumer information needs.

Having agreed the terms of reference with the sponsor, the five research groups also agreed that each would survey the extent and forms of citizenship information needs within their own national contexts as well as undertake cross-cutting thematic studies focused on specific issues, including the role and implications of new ICT-based information systems.

It was agreed that each of the national reports should:

a) outline distinctive national conceptions and traditions related to information and citizenship issues;

b) outline current issues and debates concerning information and citizenship;

c) summarise national citizenship information service provisions, functions and policies;

d)   develop appropriate practical measures of the extent and major forms of manifest citizenship information needs and examine the issue of potential or latent citizenship information needs;

e)   identify gaps between manifest need and supply of such information in the five EU Member States under study;

f)   review the application and implications of new ICTs and ISH-related themes and issues.

It was agreed that the major thrust of the empirical work would be based on interviews with relevant organisations in each of the five countries under study: both State-funded and voluntary not-for-profit organisations directly involved in the provision of citizenship information, as well as associations and organisations representing groups actively involved in citizenship information policy issues in the selected Member States.

CONCEPTIONS OF INFORMATION AND CITIZENSHIP RIGHTS AND NEEDS

In this section, I will summarise the research team's approach and findings related to conceptual and especially operational definitions of citizenship and information needs.

Defining Citizenship Information

The research team explored many different conceptual, academic and other definitions of citizenship and citizenship information rights, needs and requirements. The team also sought to develop a definition which could be operationalised for the purposes of the empirical research. These and related concerns are summarised in the following paragraphs.

In general, it was agreed that most classic theories of citizenship focus on three elements: civil, political and social. All these elements involve certain rights and responsibilities for both the individual and the State. And they require (or imply) open, and a high degree of equal, access to information if they are to be fulfilled.

Each of these elements involves wide-ranging rights, including: political rights, such as voting, accountability, participation; social rights to services and benefits; civil rights such as freedom of speech and formal legal equality. They also imply citizenship responsibilities such as compliance with laws, payment of taxes, jury service, etc.

In moving towards a definition, which could be operationalised for the purposes of the research project, the points listed below provide a summary of the approach and procedures adopted by the research team.

• At an initial and more general level, 'citizenship information' can be defined as all types of information which relate to the relationship between the individual and the State.

• In complex modern societies and electoral democracies citizens require access to an increasing amount of information participate effectively.

• In modern electoral democracies, the mass media are assumed to have the function of providing many common elements of such citizenship information.

• However many forms of information requirements, needs and responsibilities are peculiar and specialised (bespoke); they refer to particular categories of citizens and the specifics of their individual or group situation. It is this category of citizenship information that is of most concern to this study.

• The details of individual rights and responsibilities vary between EU Member States, reflecting the specifics of inherited political, civil and social structures. Nevertheless, in most EU States it was broadly accepted that citizenship involves civil, political, and social components, each involving rights and responsibilities (for which information access is critical). It should be noted that the reasons for national variations have little to do with the absence or presence of a written constitution. They largely arise from national differences in the historical development of citizenship. In particular, countries with a strong welfare state tradition generally, have well established patterns of information provision to support such citizen rights and entitlements.

• In the EU context, citizenship is primarily national; EU membership brings certain additional but complementary rights (e.g. freedom of movement, right to work and claim social security in different States) but no direct responsibilities for citizens.

• However, it is also possible to identify elements of a broadly similar pattern in all Western European States, (e.g. the idea of citizenship as having political, civil and social components). Some members of the research team were also concerned to stress the nature and extent of a distinctive 'European' conception and approach, which has tended to stress citizenship, social rights and entitlements.

Defining Citizenship Information 'Needs'

Not surprisingly perhaps, the research team encountered major difficulties in arriving at conceptual and operational definitions of citizenship information 'needs'. Below are some of the relevant highlights of the approach adopted and findings of this study.

- For present purposes, citizenship information needs (CIN) may be defined as 'the informational prerequisites for successful, and if necessary, critical participation in a social form of life'.

- One major difficulty here is that it must be recognised that individual citizens frequently may be unaware of their own relevant information needs. For example, many interviewees stressed that their clients are very often not conscious of their rights, entitlements or duties. Many citizens are also unaware that information could help them.

- Thus a large segment of citizen information needs is often unconscious and not expressed in any manifest demands. This category may be defined as latent or 'potential' citizenship information needs. Some have used the distinction between 'subjective' and 'objective' needs in this regard: the former refers to those needs of which the citizen is actually aware; the latter refers to needs which are actually required but where the citizen is not aware of their significance or implications.

By its very nature, the category of 'potential needs' is very difficult to estimate or quantify.

Main Types of Citizens' Information Needs

This classification defines the main elements of CIN which were raised by the researchers and interviewees:

a) information about civil, social and political entitlements, rights and protections;

b) information to enable participation in democratic processes and hold institutions to account; to enable critical judgement of the civil, social and political aspects of the State;

c) information on the civil, social and political responsibilities of citizenship.

Citizens and Consumers

A distinction between citizens and consumers is formally recognised in some countries (most explicitly in the Netherlands where the government assumes two types of relationship with citizens).

This distinction may be seen to give individual members of society two roles: they can be both consumers and active or participant citizens. The research team argued that individuals are both consumers and citizens, but there are many dangers in over-emphasising a strong distinction between them as these information needs may overlap (as in many cases examined in this study).

In the UK for example, the "Citizens' Charter" has generated a public debate about the relationship between the individual and public services. It has been widely criticised for constituting a consumer's charter, based on an inappropriate application of the model of the consumer of private sector services to the sphere of public services.

One useful distinction here: the consumer is the user of established public services, while the citizen has an active interest in the policy making which shapes them. This distinction is useful for understanding different forms and categories of information needs. Information about entitlements to services is predominantly the domain of the consumer; information about civil and political rights and protections is needed most by the more active and participatory citizens. Information about duties and responsibilities is needed by both citizen and consumer categories.

Thus the research team concluded that this distinction should not be overstated. But it is valid and important for:

a) understanding citizen information needs more fully;

b) evaluating existing information availability;

c) addressing important dimensions of citizenship.

CURRENT CITIZENSHIP INFORMATION NEEDS IN THE EU: SUMMARY OF THE MAIN FINDINGS

This research indicates that the informational dimensions of social exclusion and polarisation and cohesion within the EU are far from minor in scale and importance. Nor are they mere future threats or challenges associated with the advent of new ICTs or information superhighways as many recent contributions to the discourses surrounding 'Europe's way to the information society' would seem to imply.[5]

The main findings of the empirical aspects of this study were the following.

a) There is no 'market' (in the usual meaning of the word) for most citizenship information, and so 'demand' is difficult to quantify.

b) However there are a number of factors that may be taken as indicators and proxy measures of CIN and/or 'demand' in this case.

c) There is a large and growing gap between the supply of citizenship infor-

---

5. "Europe and the Global Information Society: Recommendations to the European Council. Report by Members of the High-Level Group on the Information Society" (Bangemann Report), Brussels: CEC, 1994; "Europe's way to the Information Society: An Action Plan" communication from the Commission to the Council and the European Parliament and to the Economic and Social Committee and the Committee of Regions, Brussels: CEC, 1994, COM(94) 347 final.

mation and the needs or demand for same:

(i) the citizens with greater information needs are the elderly, those on low incomes (poverty) and the disabled;

(ii) there is a strong link between unemployment and citizenship information needs;

(iii) there is also high level of CIN amongst those with least access to ICT-based technologies and skills or competencies (itself closely associated with low income and earning capacity).

d) Many existing services are already overstretched and other social, economic and demographic trends point to increasing demand for citizenship information services in the future.

e) There is very little by way of potential for the commercial information providers to meet the growing demand and gaps between supply and need in the case of CIN. It is widely accepted that most citizenship information should continue to be provided free-of-charge to the citizen as part of the status of citizenship. Besides, the ability of those with greatest needs to pay (e.g. for information about rights and services) is very limited. There is thus little possibility of charging for most types of citizenship information.

f) The greatest demand at present is for information about rights, entitlements and services. However, demand is also expected to increase for information about participation and accountability.

g) Across the EU, most citizenship information is provided by the State and its agencies. However an independent voluntary, not-for-profit sector of information and advice providers is very significant in a few countries.

h) Relatively little specific or explicit policy for citizenship information needs exists across the EU as a whole. Policy development is patchy and usually focused on one or two specific aspects or dimensions only. However citizenship information issues are becoming more of a policy concern in all EU Member States, even if this is occurring in different ways and to different extents.

i) Considerable public resources are devoted to the different forms of citizenship information provision in most Member States; but current policy reform trends may put these under increasing pressure.

THE POTENTIAL IMPACT OF NEW ICTS/ISH DEVELOPMENTS ON
CITIZENSHIP INFORMATION NEEDS

This research found that the main methods of providing citizenship information continue to be very traditional and that there is little scope for new ICT-based systems *per se* to narrow radically the gap between supply and demand for citizenship information. The following are the main findings under this heading.

1. There is a major reliance on printed material and the telephone. Most information is delivered without the citizen making use of any ICT other than the telephone.

   • Printed material is of overwhelming importance as a method of providing citizenship information, backed up by telephone services for individual inquiries and often by face-to-face information and advice provision.

   • Many categories of citizenship information needs (especially those concerned with an individual's rights and entitlements) require a human intermediary (broker) and labour-intensive, one-to-one interaction with an adviser. In the case of CIN, face-to-face information and advice provision is extremely important for those who prefer or require visits to brokers' offices or need more specialised or detailed advice.

2. In terms of the evaluation of methods of delivering citizenship information, the research highlights the importance of four main features:

   a) provision of information at a time when it is needed;

   b) provision of a personal and individualised service in which an expert adviser can help with an individual's particular case, which is required in very many situations;

   c) extensive use of printed information to back up oral information, especially to help people remember salient points;

   d) design, packaging and tailoring of up-to-date information services for the characteristic needs and requirements of specific user groups.

3. The chief uses of new ICTs in the areas relevant to citizenship information at present mainly comprise:

   a) the provision of support to the public-sector officials and independent or voluntary-agency personnel who inform and advise the public;

   b) the production of printed material (especially that tailored to specific categories of users);

   c) enhancing internal information management within the public sector services.

4. The team found that there are some well established ICT-based systems in some countries and that a range of innovations is under way, some funded under EU programmes.

    The research team sought to examine the experiences and implications of some earlier examples of ICT-based systems such as Videotex, kiosks, and teledemocracy projects.

    Videotex
    In the case of videotex, for example, the researchers examined the experience so far in the study countries. In several countries there were expectations in the early 1980s that Videotex would be widely used for this kind of application; but in most cases the expectations were not realised due to lack of investment, poor quality information provision and the lack of widespread diffusion of the system. Berlin, for example, has an extensive videotex system which still operates. It includes citizenship information which is mostly used by disabled people, advisers or brokers, and those under forty years of age. But it is significant that information about rights to welfare and so on is the least well-used part of the service.

    Teledemocracy projects
    A number of teledemocracy projects have been launched with a view to encouraging communication between citizens and their elected representatives (e.g. in the Netherlands). Most of these, however, have not been continued on a large scale because they were not considered to be financially worthwhile in terms of the amount or quality of information which was delivered and received.

    Internet
    The research team examined the more recent developments such as the Internet. The EC and member state governments are using the Internet increasingly to make certain types of information available in this way (e.g. budget statements, speeches by ministers etc). But so far this experience is largely limited to the kinds of information generally freely available through other media and press offices. The Internet has been used as the basis for more recent experiments such as the 'digital cities' projects which aim to open up new forms of communication between citizens and administrations as well as between citizens. But it is too early to make any positive assessment of the specific contribution of these newer technologies in the context of the current study.

5. The team also sought to examine the factors which may critically influence the successful use of new ICTs for the enhanced delivery of citizenship information and related future developments. The key influencing factors are listed below.

    • The willingness of governments and the EU to commit major investments in new systems will be an essential determinant of their utility. This is especially the case given that the lack of interest in CIN-related services within the private information sector and that lack of finance was a major constraint on the development of low or medium 'tech' projects within the public sector.

- In the present political climate, the route to better citizenship information may be found through governments' concerns to conduct transactions with citizens more efficiently.

- Coherent policies for citizenship information are not well developed in many countries but it is possible that technological developments and current interest in, and perceptions of, their potentialities may provide a stimulus in this regard.

- The considerable data protection concerns and related issues raised by computerised transactions need to be resolved before new systems can be fully developed and utilised.

- Whatever new systems emerge, the role of the human intermediary and adviser or interpreter will continue to be vitally important in most areas of citizenship information.

- The citizens with greater information needs are those with least access to ICT-based technologies and skills or competencies and lowest incomes. It is essential that whatever new citizenship information systems are developed, services should be available at convenient, local and public locations, i.e. not only in the home or office.

6. The research team addressed the claim that the charging of citizens for information is becoming much more viable or pressing in the light of fiscal policy trends as well as new technological developments and the perceived possibilities for expanded commercial opportunities in information provision (commodification).

    - Certainly the use of new technology raises the possibility of charging for citizenship information. This is partly because new ICT is widely viewed within the EC as opening up new prospects for the delivery of 'value-added' services across a wide range of sectors. Similar developments have occurred, with active EC financial support, in the case of 'producer' information services.

    - But this research suggests that such developments are not likely to be appropriate or viable in the case of citizenship information. As already indicated, the research team found that there is a very limited potential for the commercial information providers to fill the growing demand and gaps between supply and provision in the case of CIN. This is partly because most citizenship information should continue to be provided free of charge to the citizen as part of the status of citizenship. It is also because of the fact that the ability of those with greatest needs (e.g. for information about rights and services) is very limited. Thus an ICT-based citizenship information 'business' has little real appeal to the commercial information industry because of the lack of purchasing power in the 'market' and also because of citizens' frequent need for providers who offer in-depth knowledge and a one-to-one service.

7. As regards future developments, non-technological factors – and public policies in particular – will have greater importance than any purely technological ones in shaping developments. This is especially the case given the need to ensure equality of citizens access to appropriate information and the very nature of users' needs in this particular context. It is recognised that future technological developments are difficult to predict. It is likely that greater use of technology is likely to come about through the development of new systems for the administration of services rather than through the development of systems specifically for citizenship information provision.

CONCLUDING COMMENTS

The question of citizenship information provision and needs is one that has often featured in recent discussions of the implications of new ICTs and the NII/ISH in particular, but it has rarely been the subject of empirical investigation.

The research reported here has focused on important aspects of citizenship information exchanges and requirements which have little to do with the communication functions and content of the mass media. Thus this research has focused on some concrete aspects of information and communication processes associated with modern citizenship which have been largely neglected in many discussions of the public information sphere.

The research reported here underlines the point that citizens require access to an increasing range and diversity of information in modern electoral democracies. Indeed for their effective participation as ordinary members of advanced capitalist societies, many citizens require more than mere 'access' to such information or the carrier technologies. They also require the appropriate competencies and skills for its effective processing and utilisation (effective capacity to process and utilise the relevant information) and/or access to back-up support and broker services to achieve these ends. Clearly public libraries will continue to play a key role in certain areas of CIN, but resources did not permit an explicit examination of libraries in this study.

The research indicates that the informational dimensions of social exclusion and polarisation and cohesion within the EU are far from minor in scale and importance. Nor are they mere future threats or challenges associated with the advent of new ICTs or information superhighways as many recent contributions to the discourses surrounding 'Europe's way to the information society' would seem to imply.[6]

There is a major (and apparently growing) gap between the supply or provision of such citizen information and related back-up services within the EU. Neither new technologies, nor privatisation (commodification) policies, nor indeed the private sector are likely to provide any real solutions to these problems. A major public policy initiative on the part of national governments, complemented by the EU, is required to address this growing dimension of social exclusion and 'democratic deficits' along 'Europe's way to the information society'.

---

6. "Europe and the Global Information Society: Recommendations to the European Council, Report by Members of the High-Level Group on the Information Society" (Bangemann Report), Brussels: CEC, 1994; "Europe's Way to the Information Society: An Action Plan" communication from the Commission to the Council and the European Parliament and to the Economic and Social Committee and the Committee of Regions, Brussels: CEC, 1994. COM(94) 347 final.

REFERENCES

C Berben, "The European Framework for Competition in Telecoms" in Preston (ed.), *Competition in Telecoms Infrastructures: Proceedings of a NETEPS (Network on European Telecoms and Peripheral Regions and Smaller Entities) Workshop* COMTEC Policy Research Papers, B02.94 (Dublin: Dublin City University) 1994.

CEC, *Strategy Options to Strengthen the European Programme Industry in the Context of the Audio-visual Policy of the European Union* (Green Paper) (Brussels: CEC, COM(94) 96 final) 1994.

CEC, *Building the European Information Society for Us All: First Reflections of the High Level Group of Experts* (Brussels: CEC, Directorate General for Employment, Industrial Relations and Social Affairs) 1996.

CEC, "Information Society News" (Newsletter of the EC's Information Society Projects Office) No. 1, April 1996.

Communication Workers Union, *The Future of the Telecommunications Industry in Ireland: A Submission on Behalf of the Staff of Telecom Eireann* (Dublin: CWU) 1994.

S Deetz, Conference Theme: 'Democracy at the Crossroads' Paper to the International Communications Association Annual Conference, Albuquerque, New Mexico (ICA) 1995.

T Dignan, "Regional Disparities and Regional Policy in the EU" *Oxford Review of Economic Policy* 11(2) (1995) 64-87.

Eurostat, *Poverty Statistics in the Late 1980s* (Luxembourg: CEC) 1994.

Forfás, *Telecommunications in Ireland: A Report on Infrastructure and Services Available, Planned and Required by Irish Industry in the Period 1994-99* (Dublin: Forfás) 1994.

Forbairt, *Telecommunications, Employment and Growth: Report of the Telecommunications Industry Task Force* (Dublin: Forbairt) 1995.

H Garnham, *Capitalism and Communication* (London: Sage) 1995.

A Giddens, *Modernity and Self-identity: Self and Society in the Late Modern Age* (Cambridge, UK: Polity Press) 1991.

A Giddens, "Globalisation . . ." Keynote Address to the IAMCR (International Association for Mass Communication Research) European Conference, Dublin, June 1993 (Unpublished).

A Giddens, *A Contemporary Critique of Historical Materialism* (London: Macmillan Press) 2nd edn, 1995.

J Habermas, *The Structural Transformation of the Public Sphere* (Cambridge, UK: Polity Press) 1992.

IITF (US Government's Information Infrastructure Task Force), *National Information Infrastructure: Agenda for Action* (Washington, DC: NTIA) 1993.

ITAP (Information Technology Advisory Panel, Cabinet Office), *Making a Business of Information* (London: HMSO) 1982.

R Kavanagh, "The Government Telecommunications Network" *Seirbhís Phoiblí*, 14(3) (1994) 29-37.

H Lefebvre, *The Production of Space* (Oxford: Blackwell) English trans., 1991.

T H Marshall, *Citizenship and Social Class and Other Essays* (Cambridge, UK: CUP) 1950.

W H Melody, L Salter, & P Heyer (eds), *Culture, Communication and Dependency: The Tradition of H A Innis* (Norwood, NJ: ABLEX) 1981.

NERA, *Telecoms and Economic Development in Ireland* (London: NERA, Consultancy Report) 1993.

P Preston, "Competition in the Telecoms Infrastructure: Implications for the Peripheral Regions and Small Countries in Europe" *Telecommunications Policy* 19(4) (1995) 253-272.

P Preston & L Santiago, "Competing Visions of the ISH in Europe: Implications for Users" Paper to the PICT (Programme on Information and Communication Technologies) Conference, London, May 1995.

A Singh, et al, Special Issue on "Employment Policy in the Global Economy" *International Labour Review* No. 4/5 (1995).

J Steele (ed.), *Information for Citizenship in Europe* (London: Policy Studies Institute) 1997.

CHAPTER 7

THE CITIZEN AS INFORMATION CONSUMER AND INFORMATION SUBJECT

Roy Atkinson*

INTRODUCTION

The consumer is both a seeker of information as well as being a subject of information. The two categories overlap to a large extent, not only in the commercial world, but also in the area of public bodies. Not only do we have to consider transactions carried out for commercial reasons but also services and duties imposed by legislation.

The Freedom of Information Act is to be welcomed, but like most legislation it represents a compromise, in this case between traditions of secrecy versus desires for knowledge and openness. It also has to achieve a balance between making most information public and the right to privacy of third parties.

I will consider the provision of information as a service, the information itself as a product and approach 'freedom of information' from the traditional consumer viewpoints of full and accurate description, safety, choice, suitable means of redress and, above all, value for money.

In day-to-day consumer transactions, relations tend to be immediate and interactive and we usually have the choice of whether to deal or not with the provider of the goods or services. In dealings with public bodies the human relationships are not so clear-cut. The fact that the consumer does not usually pay at the point of receipt of service helps to foster this difference in attitude. In these cases also, we usually deal with services rather than goods. Frequently, most people are not given the choice of going elsewhere or refusing to deal with the taxman, the registry of births, marriages and deaths or, for that matter, the planning department of the local council.

---

*Roy Atkinson was the Vice-Chairman of the Consumers' Association of Ireland.

FULL AND ACCURATE DESCRIPTION
(INCLUDING MEANS OF REDRESS)

There is an information explosion, more accurately, a data explosion. The quantity held is increasing at an alarming rate, but in one sense we are running into a law of diminishing returns. Trying to sort out what is necessary and useful compared to what is surplus, duplicated and irrelevant becomes more and more difficult. Mike Cooley has often spoken about the progression from data to information, to knowledge, to wisdom. The arbitrary divisions, which for practical reasons we have to make between these concepts, become almost impossible to carry out in a consistent fashion. That is why quality of information becomes the keyword. Quality deals with accuracy, truth and relevance. Consider the internet. The quantity of information available at a few keystrokes is astounding, but quite often we have to guess at its accuracy. There is also concealment of the importance of particular information by obscurity and camouflage. It is possible to hide a needle successfully in a haystack, but it is much easier and practical to hide it among a lot of other needles, all of which are apparently similar.

How do we know who is holding information about us? Obviously the people we have given it to, and nowadays we give out more information on a regular basis than we often realise. However, have they kept it to themselves or have they spread it about? Will they tell us or do they always know? What happens in the case where other people have given information about us? Will we know where to look?

Once we find what is stored about us, how easy will it be to have inaccurate, misleading or incomplete information corrected? In the Act, section 17 appears to relate only to personal information and it is not obvious what direction its practical implementation will take. This will definitely be a case of wait and see. What, for example, will happen in the case of personal and even intimate information which already can be publicly accessed by all? Take the register of births. Are we going to see caveats entered on it? Will some birth certificates need to have other documents attached to them?

SAFETY AND SECURITY

Every advance in freedom of information means that corresponding attention must be paid to the right of privacy. How safe from unwarranted interference will the information be? Has the Act introduced or strengthened any penalties against the wrongful procurement or use of personal information? Another worrying aspect is the tendency, especially in the US, for insurers or potential employers to demand that an applicant sign a waiver agreeing to allow these people to access personal records held by public bodies. Where there is a gross inequality in bargaining power or the possibility of oppression, freedom of information could well be a millstone around the individual's neck.

Accumulation of information in large databases, whether public or private, makes members of the public feel at a disadvantage compared to the bureaucrats or big business. Too many people have casually given information about themselves without keeping proper records or copies. Until now, this has probably led to worry about inconsistencies in details which could lead to unwanted attention or complications. Much of this information was probably passed on in good faith or without fraudulent intentions, but it could have stopped a person claiming for some benefit or advantage to which they may have been entitled.

CHOICE

Normally when considering a consumer transaction, choice is looked upon as an advantage. However, when the product is information the situation may not be as clearcut. Certainly in the everyday world of commercial databases, stored information, if not neutral in content, is more likely to be negative in nature. Credit reference agencies are more likely to hold records of judgments and details of defaults in repayments rather than stories of how well people fared in their financial past. In practice, consumers will probably find that the greater the number of databases, the bigger the probability of having unwelcome and unwanted information stored on them.

VALUE AND COST OF INFORMATION

Money considerations form an important component of the consumer approach. The Freedom of Information Act lays down guidelines concerning the cost of supplying information to the public. Most of these are extremely fluid and it is difficult to predict in advance how they will be applied. Will there be uniformity all over the country or will each individual body set its own rates and conditions?

To imagine some of the likely outcomes I will consider what has already happened with the Data Protection Act and the Directive on Access to Environmental Information, both of which involve access to information which previously may have been kept confidential. I will also include areas where, by statute, information had to be supplied to the public. Consider the examples of Dublin Corporation Planning Department and An Bord Pleanála. It does not cost anything to inspect a planning application at the Corporation's magnificent offices. However, there is a small catch. If the application had been determined more than five years previously, there will be a charge of £40 to have the documents produced. I am allowed to copy, by hand or by Dictaphone, the contents of application forms, accompanying letters, third party objections and reports from the planners and various internal departments. Many of these documents such as reports have to be inspected on a computer screen while standing at the public counter. Photocopies or printouts are not supplied at all for most of these even if payment is offered. The main exception is a photocopy of the grant of permission. For this copy, which for most applications is two pages long, the price is £6.50. We are told that it is a certified copy, even though we usually do not need this added attraction.

For the plans and drawings the position is more complicated. No copies are allowed, the reason cited is that of copyright. A member of the public may not use a camera or even carbon paper or tracing paper. However, it is permissible to sketch a rough outline, take accurate measurements using a scale rule, and thus have the possibility of reconstructing the drawing at leisure. This apparent obstacle course causes the suspicion that sometimes arises that public bodies can be less than helpful in enabling enquirers to bring information away with them as opposed merely to inspecting it *in situ*.

On the other hand An Bord Pleanála will photocopy documents other than plans and drawings for ten pence per page, but you cannot inspect current appeals, only the post-mortem versions of determined appeals. At this stage, it is probably too late as the issues have been decided and cannot be re-opened except on a point of law and this is a very rare happening.

We also have to be on the alert for legislation which gives with one hand but takes away important rights with the other. There were understandable concerns with the speed of An Bord Pleanála's decision making, so legislation was introduced to reduce delays. It also severely reduced the flow of information available, especially in the case of third-party appeals. Formerly, a third-party appellant was provided by post with copies of all submissions made to the Bord concerning the appeal. Now, the entire appeal must be contained in a single submission. There is no longer an entitlement to see or comment upon other observations and submissions, even if completely new points are raised. Nor is there an opportunity to raise doubts about the accuracy of what may be presented as statements of fact. Often, the matters are wrongly accepted at face value because a contrary voice cannot be heard.

In the planning situation, it is fairly easy to keep track of documents in their folders or on bulk storage media, so there is very little time spent by staff in trying to locate them. For other types of information held by public bodies it may not be as easy to get the details to hand. If search time is always going to be charged for at an economic rate, the cost alone may make it impossible to access the information.

In applications under the Data Protection Act, which applies only to computer-based information, the search can be carried out in seconds at the effort of a few key strokes. The current maximum charge of £5 has effectively become the normal charge, at any rate insofar as credit reference agencies are concerned. More annoying again is the imposition of the full charge even if no information had been stored.

COMPARISONS WITH THE DATA PROTECTION ACT:
POSSIBLE LESSONS TO LEARN

The Data Protection Act dealt with questions of the relevance and quantity of information and the fact that it should not be held longer than necessary. Perhaps something similar is needed for some categories of information held by public bodies?

We have also seen that furnishing data as required by law can be treated as a revenue gathering exercise where the price charged may have little connection with the time and effort required. This temptation should be strongly resisted. The Data Protection Act did not have to consider the question of costs for manual documents but the ways the costs for computerised information were handled should put us on our guard.

The Data Protection Act has the loophole of manual files where personal information can be stored with no right of access. This question should be re-addressed.

The Directive on Access to Environmental Information has also shown-up some weaknesses in the question of inspection of information versus making copies of information.

PRACTICAL DIFFICULTIES STILL BEING FACED

Release of information whether personal or officially available to the public still has too many of the elements of an obstacle race; finding out who holds it, how much they hold, how much is relevant, what practical formalities have to be complied with, how much it will cost. Some personal experience under the Data Protection Act where only partial information was provided to me can bear this out.

Information can be promised repeatedly by public bodies but not supplied within suitable time limits. This happened as for example about a year ago when the Consumers' Association of Ireland requested information from the Department of Agriculture concerning antibiotic residues in pork. The official figures were only produced when the Consumers' Association had carried out an independent sampling and analysis as part of a Europe-wide investigation.

There is a danger if public bodies contract out their data processing operations. Although the Act will still apply, it may not be as easy to supervise its operation in practice. Large amounts of information have been regularly transferred abroad in the private sector. We only need to look at the example of the 'loyalty cards' recently introduced by Dunnes Stores and Quinnsworth where information concerning customer purchases is stored and analysed in the UK.

There are also details that will have to be clarified. When is a record or document to be considered as a draft or non-finalised or non-collated as opposed to a complete record or document? What is the status of "advice"? What happens where there is missing information?

The Act is a welcome addition for those who wish to see transparency and openness in the way public bodies carry out their business. However, its utility will finally depend on the way it will operate in practice. Only time will tell.

CHAPTER 8

FREEDOM OF INFORMATION IN IRELAND: AN IDEA FOR WHICH THE TIME HAS COME?

Bernadette Kennedy*

The arrival of the Freedom of Information Bill onto the Irish legislative land-scape has been acknowledged to be genuinely radical. It began life in a cultural and administrative environment that was widely recognised to be highly secretive. This 'culture of secrecy' has been influenced by a number of factors, primarily the Official Secrets Act, but also the Ministers and Secretaries Act, Dáil procedures and rules governing cabinet confidentiality.

This paper is concerned with the evolution of the Freedom of Information Bill within the Irish policy landscape. I am specifically interested in examining the pre-decision stage of the Bill – rather than with an examination of the merits and faults of the legislation itself.

The highly secretive information environment in this country has produced a tendency to underestimate the role and value of information. But despite the fact that 'information policy' has not been put on the same level as the traditional policy areas, (such as health or education policy) it cannot be considered to be a revolutionary new area. Governments have been concerned with the formulation of information policies since the evolution of the modern State. The aim has been to organise and govern their information services on a national basis, so as to satisfy a number of needs – those of citizens, the State and the administration. The fact that these policies have not been formulated with the unified vision of a national information policy does not deny their existence.

But, in this country, despite the advent of the information age and the refinement of the policy process, the information policy arena has not been analysed to any great extent. The array of speakers here today would suggest

---

***Bernadette Kennedy** obtained a Masters degree in Library and Information Studies at the Department of Library and Information Studies, UCD in 1996. She currently works with Trócaire, as Lenten Campaign Co-ordinator.

the importance of placing policies concerning the control and flow of information centre-stage in the realm of public policy.

I would argue that the arrival of the Freedom of Information Bill indicates a growing awareness of the role and value of information at a social and political level. The legislation can be considered to be a basic articulation of Ireland's emerging information regime, and it will define and redefine the policy arena as it develops within the coming years.

I would argue that existing models of public policy do not pay sufficient attention to the agenda-setting stage of the policy process. Typically, these models will focus on a particular policy initiative after it has been enacted – its life prior to this is rarely examined.

Indeed, many policy initiatives have been explained away as "an idea for which the time has come". Whilst this notion does capture "a fundamental reality about an irresistible movement that sweeps over our society"[1] it tends to mask a myriad of tensions and processes that lie behind the emergence of a particular policy.

This is particularly true for information policy. Information means different things to different people at different times. The policy arena is the scene of great conflict, and interdependency but also negotiation. The claims and agendas of the citizen, the administration, the polity, the media and industry are in constant competition and each group's success is dependent upon the types of resources that they can mobilize.

Thus, we must recognise the need to investigate the context of policy formulation, and it must also be recognised that in the contemporary nation-state, policy makers do not operate in a vacuum. They do not function as a neutral administrative body.

Any inquiry into the policy process must be firmly grounded in the pre-decision phase of policy making, agenda setting and manipulation.

As one policy analyst put it:

> The patterns of public policy, after all, are determined not only by such final decisions as votes in legislatures, or initiatives and vetoes by presidents, but also by the fact that some proposals emerge in the first place and others are never seriously considered.[2]

Within this context, it is useful to look at the work done by John Kingdon, who conducted a study of health and transportation policy in the US in the late 1970s. Kingdon's analysis provides a rich picture of the agenda-setting procedure which I find useful in investigating the emergence of the freedom of information legislation.

---

1. Kingdon, *Agendas, Alternatives and Public Policies* (Washington: Little Brown and Co) 1985, p. 1.
2. *Ibid.*, p. 2.

Kingdon set out to examine why an idea's time comes when it does. He drew a simple picture of public policy making, seeing the process as a flexible, interrelated area of activity that is in a constant state of negotiation.

He described the agenda as:

> . . . the list of subjects or problems to which governmental officials . . . are paying some serious attention at any given time.[3]

Within this he identified the government agenda as "the list of subjects that are getting attention"[4] and the decision agenda as "the list of subjects that are up for active decision".[5]

He argued that a set of alternatives for action exist in a separate arena, as alternative responses to the subject or problem on the agenda. These have a life and motion outside of the government agenda and they operate independently of each other.

But when describing the process of policy formation, we must recognise that there are pitfalls involved in trying to pinpoint the exact origins of a particular initiative. In order to understand policy, we must look at what makes a particular initiative take hold and grow, rather than become preoccupied with trying to establish the point of origin.

This series of agenda items and alternatives will be affected by a number of forces, which Kingdon identified as:

- problems;

- policies/participants;

- politics.[6]

Items will rise and disappear from the agenda depending upon the combinations and recombinations of these three separate processes. Kingdon called this mixture the "policy primeval soup".[7]

The first of Kingdon's forces is *problems*. The recognition and definition of an issue as a problem is crucial to its place within the agenda. A problem will be recognised by indicators (which are common, due to the widespread monitoring of events in modern societies), by focusing events (either personal experience or a disaster) or by feedback (which occurs within the normal chain of events in the administration of policy – one process through which civil servants will gain specialised knowledge about a subject).

The definition of an issue is also important. If a proposal is to become

---

3. *Ibid.*, p. 3.
4. *Ibid.*, p. 4.
5. *Ibid.*, p. 4.
6. *Ibid.*, p. 121.
7. *Ibid.*, p. 91.

prominent on the agenda, it will have to be linked to a problem that is real and important.

The second force is *participants* or *policies*. Ideas and proposals float around communities of specialists prior to their arrival onto the agenda. Various participants within the legislative and policy communities have differing degrees of influence over the agenda-setting process. For instance, politicians (actors who, unlike non-governmental participants, are highly visible within the process) are important in shaping the agenda, whereas invisible actors, such as academics and civil servants will have more of an effect on the specification of alternatives (in that they have the time and expertise needed to frame and test alternatives, which is, typically, a long-term process).

The final force is *politics*. The political arena has a life and dynamic of its own. Politics has a huge role to play at the drafting and implementation stages, but equally so, the ebb and flow of political life will shape the agenda. The influence of national mood, the threat or promise of elections, a changing administration or the activities of pressure groups will place certain issues in certain places within the governmental and decision agendas.

Each of these streams functions independently of the others, but at various stages, when one is amenable to another, they will combine, either in couples or all three together. For instance, if a policy actor can suggest a solution to a particular problem, then the two streams are coupled and the initiative has a chance of appearing on the government agenda. The arrival of the issue onto the decision agenda however, will have to be facilitated by the convergence of all three streams.

I would argue that freedom of information has been placed on the decision agenda of the Irish government due to the coincidence of these three processes.

A brief examination of the formation of the freedom of information proposals might suggest that the initiative originated with Eithne Fitzgerald, who has been widely associated with the Bill. But whilst she has had a highly visible and acknowledged place within the Executive, she has been but one in a complex combination of factors which has moved freedom of information into agenda prominence. She has been but one among many actors who were operating within many contexts, under the influence of many different processes.

I will now identify some of these contexts and factors. A number of political events occurred in the early 1990s which emphasised the problems that can be generated by a culture of secrecy. These include the Beef Tribunal, the Fr Brendan Smyth affair, the secrecy surrounding the tax amnesty and the alleged sale of passports to foreign investors. These events contributed to the collapse of the Fianna Fáil/Labour Government and ushered in the Rainbow Coalition and executive promises of "government through a pane of glass". As such, these events were crucial to the recognition and definition of the problem of official secrecy.

They also generated an expressed desire for open government at a societal level and this desire was manifested at a political level by the need to introduce freedom of information legislation.

These focusing events combined with elements within the political and policy streams – the advent to power of a liberal Irish government (Fine Gael, Labour Party and Democratic Left), the role of Eithne Fitzgerald within this government, and the adoption of the issue by the National Union of Journalists, and the high profile anti-censorship group – "Let in the Light".

I would argue that this combination of issues:

- the articulation of a problem;

- shifting ideologies;

- changing administrations;

- the sensing of a national mood;

- media reaction;

- election results;

- the suggestion of a viable alternative.

can be described in Kingdon's words as the appearance of a policy window.[8]

This combination enabled the notion of freedom of information to 'hit' or 'catch on' and placed the legislative proposals high on the decision agenda of the Irish government.

The context within which these proposals were formed affected the implementation and evaluation of the Bill. Thus, I would argue that it is essential to look at the agenda-setting process if we wish to gain a full understanding of information policy as it emerges as a defined field within Irish society.

---

8. *Ibid.*, p. 122.

CHAPTER 9

WHAT THE FOI ACT DOES NOT PROVIDE: A JOURNALIST'S VIEW

Michael Foley*

The Freedom of Information Act is one of the most radical pieces of legislation passed in many years. This is so because it is designed to change a culture: the Irish culture of secrecy. It is, however, disappointing to find that it has done nothing to enhance the role of a free press or to recognise the role of the press as a watchdog, as recognised by the European Court of Human Rights.

If we wanted to find an actual event from which to date the inevitability of the Freedom of Information Act we would go back to that day in January 1992 when Mr Justice Hamilton said during the Beef Tribunal, "I think that if the questions that were asked in the Dáil were answered in the way they are being answered here, there would be no necessity for this inquiry and a lot of money and time would have been saved." Mr Justice Hamilton was not to know at that time that his Tribunal would carry on hearing evidence until June 1993, would not report until August 1994, and that it would cost £35 million.

Politicians constantly talk of the Beef Tribunal as a major mistake which must never be allowed to happen again. The public interest demands that. But who is to say that the general election, the three Supreme Court cases, the investigation by a parliamentary committee, a disciplinary hearing by the Bar Council and the Freedom of Information Act were not in the public interest? All were a direct consequence of the Beef Tribunal.

Events at the Beef Tribunal led to the general election that brought in the Fianna Fáil/Labour Coalition. The Tribunal itself gave a rare glimpse of the secret working of the State, opening the door just a fraction, but enough to make it difficult to close it fully again. It was the Tribunal that made it possible for freedom of information to be added to the Programme for Government in 1993.

We are all aware of the legacy of secrecy that we inherited. In order to understand the enormity of the promise of the Freedom of Information Act it

---

*Michael Foley is the Media Correspondent of *The Irish Times* and a founder member of the anti-censorship organisation, 'Let in the Light'.

must be understood that the Irish State is one of the most secretive states in Europe, even more so than the UK. The Irish version of the Official Secrets Act is not just an inheritance from a colonial past, but was even tightened up by Fianna Fáil in 1962 giving government ministers the final say on whether information is secret or not. The then Minister for Justice, Charles Haughey, cited the need to ensure the integrity of the Leaving Certificate papers as one of the justifications. It was further fuelled by the anti- Communism of the time and the IRA campaign of a few years previously.

In essence the Irish State operates on the basis that all official information is presumed secret unless otherwise stated. This is very all-embracing. It means all documents coming out of government are secret. In this way, even the menu in the restaurant in Leinster House could be considered an official document covered by the Official Secrets Act. The Freedom of Information Act is designed to reverse that culture, putting in place a system that means everything is public unless it comes within a series of exceptions that are listed. Official secrecy is only one factor within a range of instruments ensuring secrecy. Even the guarantee of freedom of the press in the Constitution is so heavily circumscribed by considerations of public order, morality and the authority of the State as to make it almost useless. Marie McGonagle of UCG wrote in 1992 of legislation relating to free speech as being a complex web that was in need of urgent reform. Despite the Freedom of Information Act, that reform is still needed.

"No comment and don't quote me" may be the apocryphal response of the government spokesman but the effect of secrecy is such that journalists often publish second-rate information as if it was the Watergate Tapes, precisely because it is secret. In a rational world such information would probably not deserve publication at all, but in Ireland, where everything is secret that fact alone warrants that it be put into the public domain. When that does take place, the government then orders an internal inquiry to find the leak.

The Government formed after the collapse of the Fianna Fáil/Labour Coalition was also committed to freedom of information and left Minister Eithne Fitzgerald in charge of preparing the new legislation. I know of the work that went into preparing the legislation, of the research into how freedom of information worked in other jurisdictions, but there was a strong feeling that a change had taken place and whatever about the need to "let in the light on government" (Albert Reynolds) or "operate as if behind a pane of glass" (John Bruton), the realities were somewhat different. Whether it was that distance in time from the Beef Tribunal or simply a new government, I do not know, but a change took place and the concerns with openness of only a few years ago diminished.

The new Government seemed to thrive on secrecy. Some believed this was because there were three parties in Government. The Rainbow Coalition was described by one political journalist as "the most closed and least transparent administration in twenty years". That was the administration now charged with preparing freedom of information legislation.

It looked at one stage as if freedom of information had become lost in the Department of Justice where officials did much more than ensure they understood the provisions of the proposals. It appeared to be a stalling exercise, designed to hold up the proposals from being considered by Cabinet and hoping the Government might change in the meantime.

Ms Fitzgerald rescued her Bill. It went to Cabinet, but what began to emerge was something very different, at least in spirit, to what had been talked about only a few years before. No more talk of openness, transparency and accountability. Now the talk was of people having access to their own records and being able to correct them if they were inaccurate, of being able to see their social welfare and medical records. It was as if the whole exercise had been about a private right to individual information, rather than the public's right to know.

The first thing to go was the rights of "whistle-blowers". Originally the legislation was to include protection for a public servant who "blows the whistle" on what he or she believed was wrongdoing. A legal protection for "whistle-blowers" is a recognition that some people leak information because of conscience or a belief in democratic accountability. One thinks of Sarah Tisdall and Clive Ponting – the former went to prison and the latter was acquitted although he never denied leaking information to an opposition MP. Clearly the jury in his trial favoured his position over that of a secretive government, a lesson ours might have learnt. Even the Dáil Select Committee on Security and Legislation, hardly a radical body, recommended that a criminal prosecution should only take place after a leak if the information leaked related to the security or defence of the State, crime, criminal law enforcement or protection of life, or if the information was leaked for personal gain. Civil servants should be protected in claiming that the leak of information was in the public interest; if the State authorities disagree, then it would be up to the authorities to prove that it was *not* in the public interest.

Other countries that already offer protection include the US with its Whistle-blowers Charter and most Nordic countries. In Sweden it is an offence for a senior civil servant to suggest that an inquiry take place to find out who leaked, such is that country's belief that public documents belong to the public and not a closed world of civil servants and politicians.

In the US the Civil Service Reform Act 1978, known as the Whistle-blowers Act, thus protects civil servants from any form of retaliation, legal action or demotion if they disclose wrongdoing or malpractice. Civil servants are protected if they disclose to Congress, or through the Press, to the people, any evidence of violation of any law, rule or regulation, mismanagement, gross waste of funds, abuse of authority or any substantial or specific danger to public health or safety.

The rights to personal information, and the right to correct inaccurate information about oneself, should have always been in place. Ireland is a signatory of the European Convention of Human Rights. Its Court has ruled not just in favour of journalists' right to publish information concerning the workings of the state, but that the journalists have a duty to do so. It has recognised the role of the journalist as watchdog, so why did the Government not use the opportunity of the passing of the Freedom of Information Act to ensure that it was in line with our international obligation?

While the Freedom of Information Bill was working its slow journey through the system, a reporter, Ms Liz Allen of the *Sunday Independent*, was charged under the Official Secrets Act. She pleaded the only possible defence the Act allows, that she published the information, already widely available in a Garda bulletin, in the interests of the State. When the Freedom of Information Bill was published, without the Whistle-blowers Charter included, a senior civil servant suggested to me that the provision contained in the Official Secrets Act, the defence of having acted in the interests of the State, would be enough for civil servants seeking protection. Ms Allen lost her case.

It would be wrong to suggest that the Act will bring no benefits to journalism. It does reverse the long-held view that everything is secret unless otherwise stated, but what has now become law is a long way from what was promised way back in 1993 when Ms Fitzgerald actually asked if Irish journalists were up to the challenge of freedom of information at a conference organised by 'Let in the Light'. If it were to challenge journalists it would have to be less grudging. If it were to create an environment that mirrored the rulings of the European Court of Human Rights, that sought genuine openness and transparency and the public right to know the workings of government, then something more would be needed, something that showed an understanding of the role of the media in a modern democracy, an understanding that freedom of information was the plank on which a whole range of rights would be built, from the right to protect sources, to reform of the defamation laws. Instead, the Taoiseach, Mr Ahern, said at a summit meeting of the European Council in Strasbourg that he had no intention of introducing the European Convention of Human Rights into Irish law. If the UK does, as promised, bring it into their law this year Ireland will be the only EU country that has not brought the Convention into its domestic law. The reason is probably related to Article 10 of the Convention and its strong defence of freedom of expression and freedom of the press.

We also have that other legacy of the Beef Tribunal – cabinet confidentiality. Four years ago when Ms Fitzgerald was asked to prepare freedom of information legislation it looked as if this country was at last growing up. Not long ago a confused electorate allowed the Government to convince it that cabinet confidentiality should be copper-fastened and for the first time the word 'secret' entered our Constitution, according to the Irish-language version at any rate. A report prepared by the Select Committee on Legislation and Security recommended that most of the Official Secrets Act be abolished. In the brave new world of Freedom of Information it had no place. It was anachronistic and should not be part of a modern democracy, the Chairman suggested. The Freedom of Information Act came into effect in April 1998. As to when the Government will abolish the Official Secrets Act, I for one, am not holding my breath.

BIBLIOGRAPHY AND NOTES

SELECT BIBLIOGRAPHY

T Barrington, "Why is the Irish Citizen so Deprived?" *Ireland: A Journal of History and Society* 1(1) (1995) pp. 44–54.

R S Baxter, "Public Access to Business Information Held by Government" *Journal of Business Law* (May 1997) pp. 199–219. (International comparisons.)

P Birkinshaw, "Freedom of Information and Open Government and the European Community/Union Dimension" *Government Information Quarterly* 14(1) (1997) pp. 27–49.

J Black, "Official Secrets" *SCOLAG* 199 (1993) pp. 56–57.

E Cahill, "Corporate Governance and Accountability: The Information Gap in Ireland" *Ireland: A Journal of History and Society* 1(1) (1995) pp. 91–102.

A E Cawkell, "Freedom of Information in Britain and the United States" *IT LINK* 9(9) (1996) pp. 3–5.

R V Cuddihy, "Freedom of Information Act: Exceptional Opportunity for the Special Librarian" *Special Libraries* 71(3) (1980) pp. 163–168.

D de Buitleir, "Lessons for Irish Policy-making" *Ireland: A Journal of History and Society* 1(1) (1995) pp. 84–90.

G Doherty, "The Ministers and Secretaries Act 1924 and the Office of the Attorney General" *Ireland: A Journal of History and Society* 1(1) (1995) pp. 58–71.

K Doran, "Freedom of Information Act 1997: A Legal Cul de Sac?" *Gazette Law Society of Ireland* 91(9) (1997) pp. 18–20. (Medical records.)

H Doran & D A Cusack, "Access to Medical Records: The Effect of the Freedom of Information Act 1997" *Medico-Legal Journal of Ireland* 3(3) (1997) pp. 106–108.

J Doyle, "Freedom of Information: Lessons from the International Experience" *Administration* 44(4) (1996–1997) pp. 64–82.

K Edwards, "The Freedom of Information Centre" *Missouri Library World* 1(1) (1996) pp. 4–5.

E Fitzgerald, "Freedom of Information: Opening Windows on our Democracy" *Ireland: A Journal of History and Society* 1(1) (1995) pp. 154–161.

D Goldberg, "Executive Secrecy, National Security and Freedom of Information in the United Kingdom" *Government Information Quarterly* 4(1) (1987) pp. 43–61.

L Halligan, "Anti-secrecy Proposals Criticised" *Financial Times* (4 February 1998) p. 10. (Proposed UK FOI legislation.)

I Hansen, "Freedom of Information in Canada and the US" *Manitoba Library Association Bulletin* (June 1986, issued June 1987).

R Hazell, "Freedom of Information in Australia, Canada and New Zealand" *Public Administration* 67(2) (1989) pp. 189–210.

A Horton, "Freedom of Information and Public Interest Movements" in J E Brown (compiled) *LAA/NZLA Conference Proceedings* (Sydney: Library Association of Australia) 1981, pp. 296–302.

A Hyland, "The Irish Educational System and Freedom of Information" *Ireland: A Journal of History and Society* 1(1) (1995) pp. 103–109.

Irish Council for Civil Liberties, *Proposals for a Freedom of Information Act and on Open Meetings (Public Bodies) Act* (Dublin: ICCL) 1982.

Irvine of Lairg, Alexander Andrew Mackay Irvine, Lord Chancellor, "Constitutional Reform and a Bill of Rights" *European Human Rights Law Review* 5 (1997) pp. 483–489.

D Jacoby, "Recent Developments in US Federal Freedom of Information Law" *International Pension Lawyer* 15(3) (1990) pp. 84–87.

M Johnson: "Letting in the Light" *Gazette Law Society of Ireland* 91(5) (1997) pp. 16–17.

D Keogh, "Ireland and 'Emergency' Culture: Between Civil War and Normalcy 1922–1961" *Ireland: A Journal of History and Society* 1(1) (1995) pp. 4–43.

C Kimber, "Hart Workshop 1997: Access to Justice and Freedom of Environmental Information" *European Business Law Review* 8(5–6) (1997) pp. 157–164.

J Lee, "Towards Open Democracy?" *Ireland: A Journal of History and Society* 1(1) (1995) pp. 55–57.

N Marsh (ed.), *Public Access to Government Held Information* (London: Stevens) 1987. (Includes chapters on FOI in different jurisdictions.)

M McDonagh, *Freedom of Information* (Dublin: Round Hall, Sweet & Maxwell) 1998.

M McDonagh, "Access to Official Information in Ireland. Part 1: Legal Constraints on Disclosure of Information" *Irish Law Times* 13 (1995) pp. 182–186.

M McDonagh, "Access to Official Information in Ireland. Part 2: Freedom of Information" *Irish Law Times* 13 (1995) pp. 206–210.

M McDonagh, "Freedom of Information and Privacy: The Australian Experience" *Ireland: A Journal of History and Society* 1(1) (1995) pp. 136–144.

M McDonagh, "Freedom of Information in Europe" *Ireland: A Journal of History and Society* 1(1) (1995) pp. 119–125.

M McDonagh, "Access to Public Information: A Key to Commercial Growth and Electronic Democracy – Stockholm: Review" *Journal of Information Law and Technology* (1996) (http:/elj.warwick.ac.uk/elj/jilt/confs3access/).

D Meehan, "Access to Information on the Environment Under Irish and EC Law. Part 1: Minimum Standards from Europe" *Irish Law Times* 12 (1994) pp. 85–90.

D Meehan, "Access to Information on the Environment Under Irish and EC Law. Part 2: Specific Domestic Statutory Rights" *Irish Law Times* 12 (1994) pp. 114–121.

D Meehan, "Freedom of Information 1997: Public and Private Rights of Access to Records Held by Public Bodies" *Irish Law Times* 15 (1997) pp. 178–183.

D Meehan, "The Freedom of Information Act in Context" *Irish Law Times* 15 (1997) pp. 231–235.

J Michael, "Freedom of Information in Europe and Public Access to Information" in M Blake (ed.) *Proceedings of the Institute of Information Scientists Annual Conference: The Common Market for Information* (London: Taylor Graham) 1992, pp. 90–106.

L Miles, "Sweden: A Relevant or Redundant Parliament?" *Parliamentary Affairs* 50(3) (1997) pp. 423–437.

M Mills, "Freedom of Information in Ireland and the Office of the Ombudsman" *Ireland: A Journal of History and Society* 1(1) (1995) pp. 80–83.

D G Morgan, "Legal Reform, Governmental Responsibility and Freedom of Information" *Ireland: A Journal of History and Society* 1(1) (1995) pp. 110–118.

C Mullany, "Implementation of the EC Directive on Freedom of Access to Information in Ireland and Other Member States" *Irish Law Times* 12 (1994) pp. 138–144.

P E Murphy, "The United States and the Right to Know" *Ireland: A Journal of History and Society* 1(1) (1995) pp. 145–153.

F O'Toole, "Questions and Answers: Secrecy in Dáil Éireann" *Ireland: A Journal of History and Society* 1(1) (1995) pp. 72–79.

Y Poullet, "The Commercialisation of Data Held by the Public Sector" *Computer Law and Security Report* 9(5) (1993) pp. 227–233.

H C Relyea, "US Freedom of Information Act Reforms – 1986" *Journal of Media Law and Practice* 9(1) (1998) pp. 6–12.

H C Relyea et al, "Freedom of Information Developments around the World" *Government Publications Review* 10(1) (1983) pp. 1–87.

T Riley, "Developments in Freedom of Information Internationally" *Canadian Library Journal* 38 (1981) pp. 137–141.

T Riley, "A Review of Freedom of Information Around the World" *Journal of Law and Practice* 5(1) (1982) pp. 5–3.

T B Riley, "Freedom of Information in Other Jurisdictions [outside Canada]" *Journal of Media Law and Practice* 9(3) (1988) pp. 89–90.

S Roberts & I Rowlands, "Freedom of Information: A Practical Perspective" *Policy Studies* 12(2) (1991) pp. 40–51.

B Ryan, *Keeping us in the Dark: Censorship and Freedom of Information in Ireland* (Dublin: Gill & Macmillan) 1995.

R M Schmidt & R C Burns, "The Freedom of Information Act: An Overview for Librarians" *Journal of Library Administration* 7(4) (1986) pp. 9–17.

D Scott, "Freedom of Information and the European Parliament" *Ireland: A Journal of History and Society* 1(1) (1995) pp. 126–135.

J Sibbald, "Information and the Citizen: A Two-way Street" Inaugural Conference of the Coalition for Public Information *Law Librarian* 28(2) (1997) pp. 92–95.

E J Sinrod, "Specific Recommendations for Improving Media Access to Government Information" *Journal of Media Law and Practice* 15(3) (1994) pp. 79–88.

M Smith, "Freedom of Information: The UK Lags Behind" *Round Table* 283 (1981) pp. 243–252.

P Smyth & R Brady, *Democracy Blindfolded: The Case for a Freedom of Information Act in Ireland* (Cork: Cork University Press) 1994.

W G Stiles, "Freedom of Information and our State Libraries" *Canadian Library Journal* 37 (1980) pp. 391–394.

C Tapper, "Freedom of Information: A Conceptual Morass" *Information Technology and Public Policy* 12(1) (Winter 1993) pp. 40–49.

G D S Taylor, "Freedom of Information in Australia and New Zealand" in *Libraries after 1984: Proceedings of the LAA/NZLA Conference Brisbane, 1984*

(Sydney: Library Association of Australia) 1985 pp. 111–120.

P B Tetro, "Freedom of Information in Canada: An Undiscovered Resource" *International Pension Lawyer* 15(3) (1990) pp. 80–83.

I Thomson, "Transparency and Openness" [Bibliography] *European Access* 6 (1997) pp. 31–35.

N Timmins, "Confidentiality Safeguards Urged" *Financial Times* (3 February 1998) p. 10. (Proposed UK FOI legislation.)

US Congress, Senate Committee on the Judiciary, "Electronic Freedom of Information Improvement Act 1995: Report, Together with Additional Views" (Washington DC: GPO) 1996.

"Australia – ACT: Freedom of Information Ordinance 1989" *Commonwealth Law Bulletin* 15 (1989) pp. 1115–1117.

"Australia – Freedom of Information, Exemptions, Cabinet Documents: Case Comment" *Commonwealth Law Bulletin* 18 (1992) pp. 34–36. (*Department of Industrial Relations v. Forrest* [1990] A.L.R. 417.)

"Australia – Queensland: The Freedom of Information Act 1992: Review of Secrecy Provision Exemption (Queensland Law Reform Commission Report No. 46)" *Commonwealth Law Bulletin* 20 (1994) pp. 1332–1333.

"Australia – Western Australia: Freedom of Information Act 1992" *Commonwealth Law Bulletin* 20 (1994) pp. 430–431.

"Editorial: Freedom of Information and Reporting the Courts" *Irish Law Times* 15 (1997) p. 73.

"Editorial: Journalists, Confidentiality and the Right to Information" *Irish Law Times* 14 (1997) p. 273.

"Editorial: The Ombudsman, Freedom of Information and Public Bodies" *Irish Law Times* 13 (1995) pp. 181–182.

"Environmental Information" *Eurlegal* 31 (1993) p. 2. (Irish implementation legislation.)

"European Government: EU Council Shutters Closed" *Business Law Europe* 97(15) (1997) pp. 2–3.

"Freedom of Information: 'Landmark' Act will Change Britain" *Media Lawyer Newsletter* 9 (1997) pp. 1–4.

JOURNALS OF INTEREST
articles too numerous to include in the above list

Freedom of Information Review (bi-monthly)
Legal Service Bulletin Company Ltd
c/o Monash University
Faculty of Law
Wellington Road
Clayton
Victoria 3168
Australia.

Freedom of Information – Updates (Irregular)
Law Press (Victoria)
52–58 Chetwynd Street
W Melbourne
Victoria 3003
Australia.

FOI Focus Newsletter (quarterly)
Freedom of Information Foundation of Texas,
400 S. Record Street, 6th floor,
Dallas
Texas 75202
USA.

FOIA Update (Freedom of Information Act 1979)
US Department of Justice
Office of Information and Privacy
Constitution Avenue & Tenth Sts
NW Washington DC 20530-000
USA.

CASE NOTES

Case T–194/94 *John Carvel & Guardian Newspapers Ltd v. Council of the European Union* **[1995] E.C.R. II–2764 (European Court of First Instance)**

Arising from Declaration 17 of the Maastricht Treaty, the Council and Commission approved a Code of Conduct (OJ 1993 L 340, p.41) on public access to Council and Commission documents. Council Decision 93/731 implements the principles of the Code (wide public access to Council documents), and lays down the conditions for access, distinguishing exceptions where access *must* be refused, and those where access *may* be refused to protect the confidentiality of Council proceedings. The Council of Ministers refused journalist Carvel access to documents relating to reports, minutes and voting records, considering itself obliged to do so on grounds relating to confidentiality of its proceedings and deliberations, and also citing its Rules of Procedure. The Court of First Instance found that the ground for refusal based on confidentiality of proceedings was discretionary and must be exercised by balancing the citizen's interest in access to documents and the Council's interest in maintaining the confidentiality of its deliberations. Further it found that the Council had failed to exercise its discretion accordingly; nor could the Council override the citizen's right under this procedure by not exercising the discretion given to it under its own Rules of Procedure.

J D

Among the articles that comment on this case are the following:

K A Armstrong, "Citizenship of the Union? Lessons from Carvel and the Guard-
    ian" *Modern Law Review* 59(4) (1996) pp. 582–588.
K J Campbell, "Access to European Community Official Information" *Interna-
    tional and Comparative Law Quarterly* 46(1) (1997) pp. 174–180.
M O'Neill, "The Right to Information in the EU" *Eurlegal* 54 (1995) pp. 1–2.
    (supplement to *Gazette Law Society of Ireland.*)
A Sprokkereef, "Access to Information" *European Environmental Law Review*
    5(1) (1996) pp. 23–28.
P Twomey, *Common Market Law Review* 33(4) (1996) pp. 831–842.
Van Calster, "The Guardian Case" *Columbia Journal of European Law* 1(3) (1995)
    pp. 537–547.
"European Court of Justice: General" *European Environmental Law Review* 6(1)
    (1997) p. 35.

Case T–105/95   *WWF (UK) v. Commission of the European Communities*
[1997] E.C.R. II–313
(European Court of First Instance)

Arising from Declaration 17 of the Maastricht Treaty, a Code of Conduct (OJ 1993 L 340, p.41) on public access to Commission and Council documents, drawn up in 1992, was adopted by the Commission in Decision 94/90. The objective is to give the public "the widest possible access to documents held by the Commission and the Council" and it specifies grounds for refusing access, including: (a) protection of the public interest (mandatory refusal) and (b) confidentiality of its proceedings (discretionary, based on the balance between the interest of the citizen in gaining access, and its own interest in confidentiality). The WWF objected to the building of a visitors' centre (using European structural funds) at Mullaghmore in the Burren National Park, by the Irish Government. The Commission investigated the project and found no breach of European environmental law, but refused WWF access to Commission documents relating to the examination. The Court of First Instance held that both the "public interest" and "confidentiality" exceptions to the Code could be jointly pleaded, but that exceptions should be interpreted in a restrictive manner, to ensure transparency of decision-making. Insofar as the Commission had relied on the ground of confidentiality, it had made no mention of any balancing of interests. The Court found that documents relating to an investigation into possible infringement by a Member State could fall within the public interest exception because of the possibility of infringement proceedings against a state (and the need to encourage frank negotiation and settlement). However, citing a mere possibility was not enough to justify a blanket refusal of access to all documents on grounds of public interest, and the Commission ought to have listed categories of document with reasons why the documents in each category could relate to possible infringement proceedings (to allow the parties to protect their rights, and the Court to review the legality of decisions). The Court annulled the refusal, awarding costs to the applicant.

J D

Among the articles that comment on this case are the following:

M De Leeuw, *European Public Law* 3(3) (1997) pp. 339–350.
T P Kennedy, "Public Access to Commission Documents" *Gazette Law Society of Ireland* 91(3) (1997) p. 30
P F Kunzlik, "Access to the Commission's Documents in Environmental Cases: Confidentiality and Public Confidence" *Journal of Environmental Law* 9(2) (1997) pp. 321–344.
D Meehan, "EC Court of First Instance: Public Access to Documents Held by EU Commission – Alleged Misuse of Structural Funds" *Irish Planning and Environmental Law Journal* 4(3) (1997) pp. 122–124.
S Payne, "Access to Environmental Information Held by European Commission" *Student Law Review* 22 (Aut) (1997) pp. 38–39.
R Macrory, "Access to Information Ruling Hits Commission" *ENDS Report* 266 (1997) pp. 49–50.
M O'Neill, "In Search of a Real Right of Access to EC-held Documentation" *Public Law* (Aut) (1997) pp. 446–454.
Simmons & Simmons: "EC law: Administration – Transparency of Community Decision-making" *European Corporate Lawyer* 18 (1997) pp. 42–43.
Van Calster: "Access to Documents (WWF)" *Columbia Journal of European Law* 3(2) (1995) pp. 283–292.
"EU Law: Access to Environmental Information" *Environmental Law Monthly* 6(4) (1997) pp. 1–2.
"Public Access to Commission Documents" *International Financial Law Review* 16(4) (1997) p. 58.
"Access to EU Documents" *Business Law Europe* 97(4) (1997) p. 13.
Environmental Law and Management 9(3) (1997) pp. 113–114.
European Environmental Law Review 6(6) (1997) pp. 195–196.

INTERNET

There are many interesting Web sites on FOI. The following Irish site contains many links to other FOI sites:
http://indigo.ie/~pwatch/foi.htm

AN BILLE UM SHAORÁIL FAISNÉISE, 1996
FREEDOM OF INFORMATION BILL, 1996

EXPLANATORY AND FINANCIAL MEMORANDUM

Purpose of the Bill
The purpose of the Bill is to provide a right of access to information held by public bodies.
Principal features of the Bill are:

- the establishment of a legal right for each person to access information held by public bodies;

- a right for each person to have personal information relating to him/herself, and held by a public body, amended where it is incomplete, incorrect or misleading;

- a presumption that official information should be available;

- an independent appeals system to oversee decisions by public bodies under the Bill.

Right of Access
The Freedom of Information Bill proposes a legal right for each person to access information held by public bodies. Each person would also be entitled to have official information relating to him/herself amended where it is incomplete, incorrect or misleading. In addition, persons would have a legal right to reasons for decisions affecting them.

The right of access to official information proposed in the Bill would be in addition to any existing rights to obtain official information.

Publication of Material by Public Bodies
To help people focus their requests for information, public bodies would be required to publish information on their structures, functions and categories of information they hold. In addition public bodies would be required to publish the internal guidelines used in making decisions.

Procedures Governing Access
The right of access would be exercised by a person asking directly for the information from the public body concerned. Public bodies would normally have up to 20 working days in which to respond to a request. Where a request is refused, reasons for the refusal and the grounds on which it is based must normally be given.

Independent Review of Decisions
Where a request for access to information under this Bill is refused, delayed, etc. or the information is edited, a person would have a right of appeal to an independent Information Commissioner. The Commissioner would have the power to issue binding decisions. In addition, the Commissioner would have a mandate to report on the operation of the Bill generally, and on compliance by public bodies, or any particular public body with its provisions. Decisions by the Commissioner could be set aside only following a decision of the High Court.

Protection of Sensitive Information
Certain exemptions are proposed so as to protect sensitive information. These exemptions are based on standard practice in other countries with Freedom of Information legislation. Most of these exemptions are not absolute and many are subject to an overall test of whether disclosure would be in the public interest. Under two exemptions, a Minister may, in the case of exempt information which is also of sufficient sensitivity or seriousness to justify him or her doing so, issue a certificate. Where such a certificate issues, a review of the decision to refuse information is undertaken by members of the Government, rather than the Information Commissioner.

Amendment of Official Secrets Act
The Bill provides for the amendment of the Official Secrets Act so that where information is released under Freedom of Information, or in good faith that its release was so authorised, such release would not contravene that Act. The Bill also provides for review by a Select Committee of the Oireachtas of the secrecy provisions in other legislation.

Arrangement of Bill

Long Title
The long title sets out the purpose of the Bill and the right of the public to obtain access to official information to the greatest extent possible consistent with the public interest and the right to privacy.

Part I – Preliminary and General
Part I contains standard provisions in relation to short title, commencement and interpretation of various terms used.

Part II – Access to Records
This Part establishes a legal right for the public to access records held by public bodies. It sets out arrangements for making requests, and determines times within which public bodies must respond, and the ways in which access may be granted. It also requires public bodies to publish information about themselves, the information they hold, and the internal rules and guidelines used in decision making. This Part also deals with deferral and refusal of access to records. It sets out procedures for internal review. It establishes rights for each member of the public to access reasons for decisions directly affecting them, and to have personal information held by a public body amended where such information is incorrect, incomplete or misleading.

Part III – Exempt Records
This Part of the Bill sets out a series of related measures to protect information relating to key areas of Government activity. Information may be protected where its disclosure could damage the security or defence of the State, international relations or law enforcement. Matters before Government or information likely to prejudice the operations of Government may also be protected. In addition, information relating to third parties may be protected where disclosure may constitute a breach of confidence, invasion of privacy or damage to commercial interests.
    Many of the protections outlined can be set aside where the public interest would on balance be better served by the disclosure than by the withholding of the records in question.

Part IV – The Information Commissioner
This Part establishes the Office of Information Commissioner. The functions and powers of the Commissioner and the procedures for review of decisions under the Bill are also set out. In addition the Commissioner is required to keep the operation of the Bill under review and may carry out investigations into procedures adopted by public bodies for the purpose of compliance with its provisions.

Part V – Miscellaneous
This Part presumes a decision to have been made in the event of failure by a public body to reply to a request, and provides for appeals to the High Court, legal protections for the release of information under Freedom of Information, exclusions from the Bill, fees and the amendment of the Official Secrets Act.
Detailed Provisions

PART I

PRELIMINARY AND GENERAL

Section 1 provides that the Bill will commence a year after enactment. On commencement the Bill will apply to all bodies listed at *subparagraphs (1)* and *(2)* of *paragraph 1* of the *First Schedule*. This section also provides that the Bill will apply to local authorities and health boards within three years of enactment.

Section 2 provides for interpretation and defines a record so as to capture information held in either electronic or any other form.

Section 3 provides for the making of regulations in implementing the Bill, including its extension to bodies in the wider public service.

Section 4 provides for delegation of functions. This enables decisions on the release of information to be taken at lower levels in a public body and the operation of an effective internal review system.

Section 5 is a standard provision relating to expenses.

PART II

ACCESS TO RECORDS

Section 6 provides a legal right for the public to official information and imposes an obligation on public bodies to assist the public when making requests for such information.

In general, access will be provided to records created from commencement of the Bill, along with access to earlier records, where these are necessary to understand more recent information. In addition the Minister for Finance can, by regulations, provide general access to records created before commencement. Personal records may be accessed regardless of when they were created. As regards personnel records of staff in public bodies, access will be available to current records or any earlier records liable be used in a way that might adversely affect the interests of the member of staff involved.

Section 7 sets out how the right of access is to be exercised and also requires that public bodies acknowledge receipt of requests within two weeks.

Section 8 requires that public bodies decide whether to accede to or refuse requests within four weeks of receipt and that they notify the requester accordingly. Where a request is being refused, reasons for refusal must be given, along with a statement setting out rights of review and appeal.

Section 9 allows the period within which a decision must be made on a request to be extended by up to four weeks if the request, or related requests, concern such a large number of records that compliance within the specified timeframe is not possible.

Section 10 sets out practical grounds for refusing a request.

Section 11 permits deferral of access to a narrow range of records, while *section 12* provides for different ways in which access can be granted. Where part of a record is exempt, *section 13* provides for access to the remainder, where this is practical and does not mislead.

Section 14 provides for internal review against an initial decision by a public body in respect of the following: refusal to grant a request; deferral of access to a document being prepared for the Houses of the Oireachtas; the provision of access in a form other than that requested; the granting of access to part only of a record; a refusal to amend a record relating to personal information; the giving of reasons for a decision; and the charging of a fee or deposit in respect of the grant of access. Such a review must be undertaken at a higher level than that at which the original decision was made, and completed within three weeks.

Section 15 requires that a public body must publish information setting out a general description of its structure, functions and services it provides to the public as well as a general description of its rules and guidelines used in implementing its schemes and programmes. In addition it must describe the classes of records it holds and the arrangements for enabling the public to access such records. The provision also requires the public body to set out rights of review and appeal against its decisions generally.

Section 16 requires that each public body publish the rules, procedures, guidelines, interpretations and an index of precedents used by it for the purposes of decisions and recommendations. Where such material is not published, or, where published, it is incomplete or inaccurate, the public body concerned is required to ensure that a person is not prejudiced, due to such failure or error on the part of that body.

Section 17 confers a legal right on each member of the public to require that personal information relating to oneself and held by a public body be amended, where it is incomplete, incorrect or misleading.

Section 18 confers a legal right on each person to reasons for a decision on a matter particularly affecting that person.

PART III

EXEMPT RECORDS

Section 19 protects matters prepared for consideration by Government and related briefing material. This protection does not apply where five or more years have elapsed since the relevant Government decision was made or where the information constitutes factual material and the decision to which it relates has been made public.

Section 20 provides that access to records relating to the deliberative processes of a public body may be refused, but only where disclosure would be contrary to the public interest. This section does not offer protection to factual information, certain technical reports or reports on the performance or effectiveness of public bodies. Internal rules and guidelines and reasons for decisions are also excluded from the protections afforded to the deliberative processes.

Under *section 21* records may be protected where disclosure could prejudice the effectiveness of certain operations of a public body. Such operations would include audit, control, examinations or investigative functions of the body. In addition, this provision offers protection in respect of industrial relations functions and negotiating positions of Government and state agencies. Information may be released where the public interest would on balance, be better served by granting than by refusing the request.

Section 22 exempts from disclosure certain matters relating to the proceedings of the Oireachtas and records which would be in contempt of court, or protected on the grounds of legal professional privilege. The private papers of elected representatives of the European Parliament and of Local or Regional Authorities are also protected. (The private papers of Oireachtas Members are excluded under *section 46*).

Section 23 provides that information may be protected where its disclosure could prejudice or impair law enforcement functions. This protection does not extend to information concerning the performance of a body or the success or otherwise of a law enforcement programme or policy where the public interest would be served by such disclosure.

Section 24 provides that information may be withheld where its disclosure could adversely affect defence, security or international relations.

Section 25 outlines the procedures in relation to the issue of Ministerial certificates. Where a Minister is satisfied that information sought is exempt by reference to prejudicing interests in *sections 23* or *24, and* that the information is of sufficient sensitivity or seriousness to justify him or her doing so, he or she may sign a certificate confirming that the material is exempt. In such cases review is undertaken by other members of the Government rather than by the Information Commissioner. A certificate must be withdrawn where such a review finds insufficient grounds for its use.

Section 26 provides that information may be protected where it has been given to a public body and is subject to an obligation of confidence. This section also provides that a public body should consult with the Information Commissioner prior to entering into classes of confidential agreements. The head has discretion to consider release of the information where, on balance, he or she is of the opinion that it is in the public interest to do so. Prior to making a decision on such release, the consultation procedures in *section 29* must be followed.

Section 27 provides that a public body may refuse to grant access to commercially sensitive information to persons other than the individual or company to whom the information relates. The head has discretion to consider release of the information where, on balance, he or she is of the opinion that it is in the public interest to do so. Prior to making a decision on such release, the consultation procedures in *section 29* must be followed.

Section 28 protects personal information held by a public body against third party access. A definition of "personal information" is included at *section 2* of the Bill. Particular procedures are specified in respect of medical or social work information where the head of the body is of the opinion that its disclosure to the person concerned may be prejudicial to his or her health or emotional well-being. In these circumstances, the public body shall, if requested to do so by the person concerned, instead release the record to an appropriate health professional nominated by the requester.

The head has discretion to consider release of the information to a third party where, on balance, he or she is of the opinion that the public interest in disclosure outweighs the right to privacy of the individual concerned or where release of the information would benefit the individual. Prior to making a decision on such release the consultation procedures in *section 29* must be followed.

Section 29 outlines consultation procedures to be followed if a head proposes to release, in the public interest, information referred to in *sections 26, 27* or *28*. In that case, the public body is obliged to:

(i)   advise the relevant third party of the intention to release the information and the public interest grounds involved,

(ii) consider the response of the third party prior to deciding on disclosure, and

(iii) allow opportunity for appeal to the Commissioner, if the public body proposes release of the information.

Section 30 deals with information relating to research and natural resources. Information in relation to research may be withheld by a public body if premature disclosure of the information would be likely to expose the body concerned or the persons engaged in the research to serious disadvantage. Information may also be protected where its release could reasonably be expected to prejudice the well-being of a cultural, heritage or natural resource or the habitat or species of flora or fauna. Information may be released where the public interest would on balance, be better served by granting than by refusing the request.

Section 31 protects information where its disclosure could reasonably be expected to have serious adverse effects for the financial interests of the State or the ability of the Government to manage the economy. Information is also protected if premature disclosure could result in undue disturbance of the ordinary course of business of the community or in undue benefit or loss to any person. Information may be released where the public interest would on balance, be better served by granting than by refusing the request.

Section 32 upholds the operation of specific secrecy provisions in other enactments. However, general "catch-all" secrecy provisions, listed in *Schedule 3,* are set aside for the purposes of FOI, in favour of the particular provisions set out in this Bill. This section further provides for periodic review of secrecy provisions in other enactments by a Committee of the Oireachtas.

Existence or non-existence of information – The head of a public body may refuse to disclose the existence or non-existence of information in certain specific circumstances. This provision may be used to protect information outlined in *sections 23(1)* (Law Enforcement) or *24(1)* (Defence, Security etc.) where disclosure of its existence or non-existence would be likely to prejudice the interests protected by those subsections. In addition this provision may be used to protect information referred to in *sections 19(1)* (Matters before Government) or *22(1)(a)* (Parliamentary, Court, etc.), where confirmation of its existence or non-existence would be contrary to the public interest

PART IV

INFORMATION COMMISSIONER

Section 33 provides for the establishment of the Office of Information Commissioner. A technical amendment to the Ombudsman Act, 1980, is proposed so as to allow for the appointment of the Ombudsman as Information Commissioner.

Section 34 outlines the decisions subject to review by the Commissioner. The Commissioner would, on review, exercise the same powers as the head of a public body and his or her decisions would be binding on the parties concerned, subject to appeal to the High Court under *section 42*. This section also provides that the onus shall be on the public body to show that its original decision to refuse information, etc. was justified.

Section 35 allows the Commissioner to require a public body to provide more detailed reasons for refusal to grant a request where he or she is of the view that the details given in a notice under *section 8* are inadequate. Such additional information may include particulars taken into account by the public body pertaining to the public interest.

Section 36 provides that the Commissioner shall keep the Bill under review and may carry out investigations into the practices and procedures adopted by public bodies for the purpose of compliance with the provisions of the Bill.

Section 37 sets out the powers of the Commissioner to examine documents and summon witnesses.

Section 38 provides that the Commissioner shall foster and encourage the publication by public bodies of information of relevance and interest to the public.

Section 39 enables the Commissioner to make available information on the practical application of the Bill, including particular provisions.

Section 40 provides for the preparation of annual and special reports by the Commissioner.

PART V

MISCELLANEOUS

Section 41 provides that failure by a public body to reply to a request within the timeframe specified will be deemed to be a refusal. Following from this the requester can proceed further to appeal.

Section 42 provides for appeal to the High Court on a point of law against a decision of the Information Commissioner, or in relation to a matter the subject of a Ministerial Certificate.

Precautions against the disclosure of exempt information and stay on certain decisions which may be subject to appeal are set out in *sections 43* and *44*.

Section 45 sets out legal protections for the granting of access to a record in accordance with the provisions of the Bill, or in the reasonable belief that its provisions were complied with.

Section 46 sets out matters which are outside the scope of the Bill. This provision relates principally to information which is constitutionally protected, or which would disclose the identity of a confidential source of information in relation to enforcement of criminal law, or which is otherwise publicly available.

Section 47 provides that fees may be charged in respect of the location and copying of records, based on a standard hourly rate, to be prescribed by the Minister of Finance. No charges will apply in relation to the location of records in respect of personal information, save where a large number of records are involved. No charges will apply: where the cost of collecting and accounting for the fee would exceed the amount of the fee; where the information would be of particular assistance to the understanding of an issue of national importance; or, in the case of personal information, where such charges would not be reasonable having regard to the means of the requester. A deposit may be charged where the fee involved is likely to exceed £40.

Section 48 amends the Official Secrets Act, 1963, by providing that a person is deemed to be duly authorised under that Act to release official information, where they do so on the basis of being so authorised under this Bill, or in the reasonable belief that he or she is so authorised. This section also provides defence against prosecution under the Official Secrets Act.

SCHEDULES

First Schedule - this schedule lists public bodies for the purposes of the Bill. Government Departments and other bodies listed in *paragraphs (1)* and *(2)* of *subsection 1* will come within the scope of the Bill on commencement. The Bill will apply to local authorities and health boards on a date to be agreed with the relevant Minister, not later than 3 years from enactment (*section 1* refers). *Paragraph (5)* of *subsection 1* allows for the designation of other public sector bodies with the consent of the relevant Minister.

Second Schedule – this schedule sets out the terms and conditions of the Commissioner.

Third Schedule – this schedule lists the general secrecy provisions which are set aside in favour of FOI exemptions for the purposes of this Bill.

Financial Implications
The estimated cost of implementation of the Bill is £2 million per annum, including publicity and training costs. Experience abroad indicates that Freedom of Information does not give rise to significant additional staffing requirements for public bodies generally. In the case of the office of the Information Commissioner the additional staffing requirement is estimated at 9 administrative, legal and clerical staff.

Oifig an Tánaiste,
Nollaig, 1996.

APPENDIX TWO

NOTE ON FEES UNDER SECTION 47 OF THE ACT

On 1 May 1998, by Regulations entitled the Freedom of Information Act 1997 (section 47(3)) Regulations 1998 (S.I. No. 139 of 1998) the Minister for Finance prescribed for the time being an amount of £16.50 per hour for time spent searching for and retrieving records. The maximum costs of providing copies are three pence per sheet for photocopying, forty pence for a 3½ inch computer disk and £8 for a CD-ROM.

APPENDIX THREE

Number 13 *of* 1997

FREEDOM OF INFORMATION ACT 1997

ARRANGEMENT OF SECTIONS

PART I

PRELIMINARY AND GENERAL

PART II

ACCESS TO RECORDS

PART III

EXEMPT RECORDS

PART IV

THE INFORMATION COMMISSIONER

PART V

MISCELLANEOUS

FIRST SCHEDULE

PUBLIC BODIES

SECOND SCHEDULE

THE INFORMATION COMMISSIONER

THIRD SCHEDULE

ENACTMENTS EXCLUDED FROM APPLICATION OF *Section 32*

PART I

STATUTES

PART II

STATUTORY INSTRUMENTS

ACTS REFERRED TO

Agriculture (Research, Training and Advice) Act, 1988	1988. No. 18
An Bord Bia Act, 1996	1996, No. 21
Bord Glas Act, 1990	1990, No. 1
Children Act, 1908	1908, c. 67
Civil Service Commissioners Act, 1956	1956, No. 45
Civil Service Regulation Act, 1956	1956, No. 46
Civil Service Regulation Acts, 1956 and 1958	
Combat Poverty Agency Act, 1986	1986, No. 14
Companies Act, 1963	1963, No. 33
Companies Acts, 1963 to 1990	
Competition Act, 1991	1991, No. 24
Comptroller and Auditor General Acts, 1923 and 1993	
Copyright Act, 1963	1963, No. 10
Data Protection Act, 1988	1988, No. 25
Defence Act, 1954	1954, No. 18
Dentists' Act, 1985	1985, No. 9
Employment Equality Act, 1977	1977, No. 16
Environmental Protection Agency Act, 1992	1992, No. 7
European Assembly Act, 1977	1977, No. 30
European Parliament Elections Act, 1993	1993, No. 30
Exchequer and Audit Department Acts, 1866 and 1921	
Forestry Act, 1988	1988, No. 26
Gas Act, 1976	1976, No. 30
Harbours Act, 1996	1996, No. 11
Industrial Development Act, 1986	1986, No. 9
Industrial Development Act, 1993	1993, No. 19
Industrial Relations Act, 1946	1946, No. 26
Industrial Relations Act, 1969	1969, No. 14
Industrial Relations Act, 1990	1990, No. 19
Irish Aviation Authority Act, 1993	1993, No. 27

Irish Film Board Act, 1980	1980, No. 36
Irish Horseracing Industry Act, 1994	1994, No. 18
Irish Medicines Board Act, 1995	1995, No. 29
Labour Services Act, 1987	1987, No. 10
Local Authorities (Officers and Employees) Act, 1926	1926, No. 39
Local Government (Planning and Development) Act, 1983	1983, No. 28
Local Government Act, 1941	1941, No. 23
Marine Institute Act, 1991	1991, No. 2
Medical Practitioners Act, 1978	1978, No. 4
Milk (Regulation of Supply) Act, 1994	1994, No. 25
Ministers and Secretaries Act, 1924	1924, No. 16
National Archives Act, 1986	1986, No. 11
National Social Services Board Act, 1984	1984, No. 2
National Treasury Management Agency Act, 1990	1990, No. 18
Offences Against the State Act, 1939	1939, No. 13
Official Secrets Act, 1963	1963, No. 1
Ombudsman Act, 1980	1980, No. 26
Pensions Act, 1990	1990, No. 25
Performers' Protection Act, 1968	1968, No. 19
Postal and Telecommunications Services Act, 1983	1983, No. 26
Public Offices Fees Act, 1879	1879, c. 58
Prisons Acts, 1826 to 1980	
Radiological Protection Act, 1991	1991, No. 9
Restrictive Practices (Amendment) Act, 1987	1987, No. 31
Roads Act, 1993	1993, No. 14
Safety, Health and Welfare at Work Act, 1989	1989, No. 7
Social Welfare Acts	
Social Welfare (Consolidation) Act, 1993	1993, No. 27
Tax Acts	
Trade and Marketing Promotion Act, 1991	1991, No. 22
Transport (Re-organisation of Córas Iompair Éireann) Act. 1986	1986, No. 31
Tribunals of Inquiry (Evidence) Act, 1921	1921, c. 7
Údarás na Gaeltachta Act, 1979	1979, No. 5
Voluntary Health Insurance (Amendment) Act, 1996	1996, No. 4

FREEDOM OF INFORMATION ACT, 1997

AN ACT TO ENABLE MEMBERS OF THE PUBLIC TO OBTAIN ACCESS, TO THE GREATEST EXTENT POSSIBLE CONSISTENT WITH THE PUBLIC INTEREST AND THE RIGHT TO PRIVACY, TO INFORMATION IN THE POSSESSION OF PUBLIC BODIES AND TO ENABLE PERSONS TO HAVE PERSONAL INFORMATION RELATING TO THEM IN THE POSSESSION OF SUCH BODIES CORRECTED AND, ACCORDINGLY, TO PROVIDE FOR A RIGHT OF ACCESS TO RECORDS HELD BY SUCH BODIES, FOR NECESSARY EXCEPTIONS TO THAT RIGHT AND FOR ASSISTANCE TO PERSONS TO ENABLE THEM TO EXERCISE IT, TO PROVIDE FOR THE INDEPENDENT REVIEW BOTH OF DECISIONS OF SUCH BODIES RELATING TO THAT RIGHT AND OF THE OPERATION OF THIS ACT GENERALLY (INCLUDING THE PROCEEDINGS OF SUCH BODIES PURSUANT TO THIS ACT) AND, FOR THOSE PURPOSES, TO PROVIDE FOR THE ESTABLISHMENT OF THE OFFICE OF INFORMATION COMMISSIONER AND TO DEFINE ITS FUNCTIONS, TO PROVIDE FOR THE PUBLICATION BY SUCH BODIES OF CERTAIN INFORMATION ABOUT THEM RELEVANT TO THE PURPOSES OF THIS ACT, TO AMEND THE OFFICIAL SECRETS ACT, 1963, AND TO PROVIDE FOR RELATED MATTERS. [21*st April*, 1977]

BE IT ENACTED BY THE OIREACHTAS AS FOLLOWS:

PART I

PRELIMINARY AND GENERAL

1.—(1) This Act may be cited as the Freedom of Information Act, 1997.

(2) Subject to *subsection (3)*, this Act shall come into operation on the day that is one year after the date of its passing.

(3) *Subparagraph (3)* of *paragraph 1* of the *First Schedule* shall come into operation on such day not later than 18 months after the passing of this Act as the Minister may appoint by order with the consent of the Minister for the Environment and *subparagraph (4)* of that paragraph shall come into operation on such day not later than 18 months after the passing of this Act as the Minister may appoint by order with the consent of the Minister for Health.

Citation and commencement.

2.—(1) In this Act, save where the context otherwise requires—

"commencement of this Act" means the time at which this Act (other than *subparagraphs (3)* and *(4)* of *paragraph 1* of the *First Schedule*) comes into operation;

"the Commissioner" means, as the context may require, the office of Information Commissioner established by *section 33* or the holder of that office;

"determined" means determined by the Minister and, in relation to a form, means determined having had appropriate regard to the needs of requesters, and cognate words shall be construed accordingly;

Interpretation.

"director" means a director (within the meaning of the Companies Acts, 1963 to 1990) but includes, in the case of a local authority or health board or any other public body that is not a company (within the meaning of the Companies Act, 1963) or, being a body, organisation or group (other than a company) specified in *subparagraph (b) (i), (c), (e), (f)* or *(g)* of *subparagraph (5)* of *paragraph 1* of the *First Schedule*, stands prescribed for the time being pursuant to that subparagraph, a person who is a member of it or a member of any board or other body that controls, manages or administers it, and any cognate words shall be construed accordingly;

"enactment" means a statute or an instrument made under a power conferred by a statute;

"exempt record" means—
>   (*a*) a record in relation to which the grant of a request under *section 7* would be refused pursuant to *Part III* or by virtue of *section 46*, or
>   (*b*) a record that is created for or held by an office holder and relates to the functions or activities of—
>   (i) the office holder as a member of the Oireachtas or a political party, or
>   (ii) a political party;

"functions" includes powers and duties and references to the performance of functions include, with respect to powers and duties, references to the exercise of the powers and the carrying out of the duties;

"give" includes send, whether by post or electronic or other means, and cognate words shall be construed accordingly;

"head" means head of a public body;

"head of a public body" means—
>   (*a*) in relation to a Department of State, the Minister of the Government having charge of it,
>   (*b*) in relation to the Office of the Tánaiste, the Tánaiste,
>   (*c*) in relation to the Office of the Attorney General, the Attorney General,
>   (*d*) in relation to the Office of the Director of Public Prosecutions, the Director of Public Prosecutions,
>   (*e*) in relation to the Office of the Comptroller and Auditor General, the Comptroller and Auditor General,
>   (*f*) in relation to the Office of the Ombudsman, the Ombudsman,
>   (*g*) in relation to the Office of the Commissioner, the Commissioner,
>   (*h*) in relation to the Office of the Civil Service Commissioners, the Civil Service Commissioners,
>   (*i*) in relation to the Office of the Local Appointments Commissioners, the Local Appointments Commissioners,
>   (*j*) in relation to the Office of the Houses of the Oireachtas, the Chairman of Dáil Éireann,
>   (*k*) in relation to any other public body, the person who holds, or performs the functions of, the office of chief executive officer (by whatever name called) of the body;

"local authority" means a local authority for the purposes of the Local Government Act, 1941;

"the Minister" means the Minister for Finance;

"Office", in relation to a person, means the offices in which the administration and business relating to the functions of the person are carried on;

"office holder" means—
>   (*a*) a person who is a Minister of the Government or a Minister of State, or

(*b*) a member of either House of the Oireachtas who holds the office of Attorney General;

"personal information" means information about an identifiable individual that—

    (*a*) would, in the ordinary course of events, be known only to the individual or members of the family, or friends, of the individual, or

    (*b*) is held by a public body on the understanding that it would be treated by it as confidential,

and, without prejudice to the generality of the foregoing, includes—

    (i)   information relating to the educational, medical, psychiatric or psychological history of the individual,

    (ii)   information relating to the financial affairs of the individual,

    (iii) information relating to the employment or employment history of the individual,

    (iv) information relating to the individual in a record failing within *section 6 (6) (a)*,

    (v)   information relating to the criminal history of the individual,

    (vi) information relating to the religion, age, sexual orientation or marital status of the individual,

    (vii) a number, letter, symbol, word, mark or other thing assigned to the individual by a public body for the purpose of identification or any mark or other thing used for that purpose,

    (viii) information relating to the entitlements of the individual under the Social Welfare Acts as a beneficiary (within the meaning of the Social Welfare (Consolidation) Act, 1993) or required for the purpose of establishing whether the individual, being a claimant (within the meaning aforesaid), is such a beneficiary,

    (ix) information required for the purpose of assessing the liability of the individual in respect of a tax or duty or other payment owed or payable to the State or to a local authority, a health board or other public body or for the purpose of collecting an amount due from the individual in respect of such a tax or duty or other payment,

    (x)   the name of the individual where it appears with other personal information relating to the individual or where the disclosure of the name would, or would be likely to, establish that any personal information held by the public body concerned relates to the individual,

    (xi) information relating to property of the individual (including the nature of the individual's title to any property), and

    (xii) the views or opinions of another person about the individual,

but does not include—

    (I)   in a case where the individual holds or held office as a director, or occupies or occupied a position as a member of the staff, of a public body, the name of the individual or information relating to the office or position or its functions or the terms upon and subject to which the individual holds or held that office or occupies or occupied that position or anything written or recorded in any form by the individual in the course of and for the purpose of the performance of the functions aforesaid,

    (II) in a case where the individual is or was providing a service for a public body under a contract for services with the body, the name of the individual or information relating to the service or the terms of the contract or anything written or recorded in any form by the individual in the course of and for the purposes of the provision of the service, or

    (III) the views or opinions of the individual in relation to a public body, the staff of a public body or the business or the performance of the functions of a public body;

"political party" means a party registered in the Register of Political Parties;

"prescribed" means prescribed by the Minister by regulations under *section 3*;

"public body" shall be construed in accordance with the *First Schedule*;

"record" includes any memorandum, book, plan, map, drawing, diagram, pictorial or graphic work or other document, any photograph, film or recording (whether of sound or images or both), any form in which data (within the meaning of the Data Protection Act, 1988) are held, any other form (including machine-readable form) or thing in which information is held or stored manually, mechanically or electronically and anything that is a part or a copy, in any form, of any of the foregoing or is a combination of two or more of the foregoing;

"request to which *section 29* applies" means a request under *section 7* to which *section 26 (3), 27 (3)* or *28 (5)* applies and which, apart from *section 29*, would fall to be granted;

"requester" means a person who makes a request under *section 7*;

"the right of access" shall be construed in accordance with *section 6*;

(2) A power conferred by this Act to draw up and publish guidelines or to make determinations shall be construed as including a power exercisable in the like manner to revoke or amend guidelines or determinations drawn up and published or, as the case may be, made under the power.

(3) Nothing in this Act shall be construed as prohibiting or restricting access by a public body to a record held by another public body.

(4) A reference in *section 7, 8, 14, 17* or *18* in relation to a request under *section 7* or the receipt of such a request or to an application under *section 14 (2), 17 (1)* or *18 (1)*, to the head of a public body shall be construed as including a reference to the body and to any director or member of the staff thereof, and this Act shall, with any necessary modifications, apply and have effect accordingly.

(5) In this Act—

    (*a*) a reference to records held by a public body includes a reference to records under the control of the body,

    (*b*) a reference to a Part, section or Schedule is a reference to a Part or section of, or a Schedule to, this Act unless it is indicated that reference to some other provision is intended, and

    (*c*) a reference to a subsection, paragraph, subparagraph, clause or subclause is a reference to a subsection, paragraph, subparagraph, clause or subclause of the provision in which the reference occurs, unless it is indicated that reference to some other provision is intended, and

    (*d*) a reference to any enactment is a reference to that enactment as amended, adapted or extended by or under any subsequent enactment.

Regulations.

3.—(1) The Minister may—

    (*a*) by regulations provide, subject to the provisions of this Act, for any matter referred to in this Act as prescribed or to be prescribed, and

    (*b*) in addition to any other power conferred on him or her to make regulations, make regulations generally for the purposes of, and for the purpose of giving full effect to, this Act,

    (*c*) if, during the first 3 years of application of this Act to a public body specified in *subparagraph (3), (4)* or *(5)* of *paragraph 1* of the *First Schedule*, any difficulty arises in bringing this Act into operation in so far as it applies to that body, by regulations do anything which appears to be necessary or expedient for bringing this Act into operation in so far as it applies to that body and regulations under this paragraph may, in so far only as may appear necessary for carrying the regulations into effect, modify a provision of this Act if the

> modification is in conformity with the purposes, principles and spirit of this Act, and
>
> (d) if in any other respect any difficulty arises during the period of 3 years from the commencement of this Act in bringing this Act into operation, by regulations do anything which appears to be necessary or expedient for bringing this Act into operation and regulations under this paragraph may, in so far only as may appear necessary for carrying the regulations into effect, modify a provision of this Act if the modification is in conformity with the purposes, principles and spirit of this Act.

(2) Regulations under this Act may contain such incidental, supplementary and consequential provisions as appear to the Minister to be necessary or expedient for the purposes of the regulations.

(3) Where the Minister proposes to make regulations under *paragraph (c)* or *(d)* of *subsection (1)* or for the purposes of *paragraph 1 (5)*, or under *paragraph 3*, of the *First Schedule*, he or she shall cause a draft of the regulations to be laid before each House of the Oireachtas and the regulations shall not be made until a resolution approving of the draft has been passed by each such House.

(4) Where the Minister proposes to make regulations under *subsection (1) (c)*, he or she shall, before doing so, consult with such other (if any) Minister of the Government as the Minister considers appropriate having regard to the functions of that other Minister of the Government in relation to the proposed regulations.

(5) Regulations prescribing a body, organisation or group ("the body") for the purposes of *paragraph 1 (5)* of the *First Schedule* may provide that this Act shall apply to the body only as respects specified functions of the body, and this Act shall apply and have effect in accordance with any such provision.

(6) Every regulation under this Act (other than a regulation referred to in *subsection (3)*) shall be laid before each House of the Oireachtas as soon as may be after it is made and, if a resolution annulling the regulation is passed by either such House within the next 21 days on which that House has sat after the regulation is laid before it, the regulation shall be annulled accordingly but without prejudice to the validity of anything previously done thereunder.

4.—(1) A head may delegate in writing to a member of the staff of the public body concerned any of the functions of the head under this Act (other than this section and *section 25*). *[Delegation of certain functions of heads.]*

(2) A delegation under *subsection (1)* ("a delegation") may—

(a) relate to functions generally or specified functions or be in respect of records generally or specified classes of records or specified records, and

(b) be to a specified member or specified members of the staff of the public body concerned or to such members who are of a specified rank or grade or of a rank or grade not lower than a specified rank or grade,

and may delegate different functions or classes of function to different such members or classes of members.

(3) A delegation may be revoked in whole or in part or amended in writing by the head for the time being of the public body concerned.

(4) A delegation shall operate, so long as it continues in force, to confer on and vest in the person concerned the function or functions delegated by the delegation.

(5) The head concerned shall cause notice of a delegation or of a revocation or amendment under *subsection (3)* to be published in *Iris Oifigiúil* not later than 4 weeks after the making of the delegation, revocation or amendment, as the case may be.

(6) References in this Act to a head shall be construed, where appropriate having regard to the context and any delegation under this section, as including references to any person to whom functions stand delegated by the delegation.

Expenses.   **5.**—The expenses incurred in the administration of this Act shall be paid out of moneys provided by the Oireachtas and the expenses incurred by any other Minister of the Government in the administration of this Act shall, to such extent as may be sanctioned by the Minister, be paid out of moneys provided by the Oireachtas.

PART II

ACCESS TO RECORDS

Right of   **6.**—(1) Subject to the provisions of this Act, every person has a right to and shall, on
access to   request therefor, be offered access to any record held by a public body and the right so
records.   conferred is referred to in this Act as the right of access.

(2) It shall be the duty of a public body to give reasonable assistance to a person who is seeking a record under this Act—

  (a) in relation to the making of the request under *section 7* for access to the record, and

  (b) if the person has a disability, so as to facilitate the exercise by the person of his or her rights under this Act.

(3) The Minister shall, after consultation with such other (if any) Ministers of the Government as he or she considers appropriate, draw up and publish to public bodies guidelines in relation to compliance by public bodies with *subsection (2)(b)*, and public bodies shall have regard to any such guidelines.

(4) The records referred to in *subsection (1)* are records created after the commencement of this Act and—

  (a) records created during such period (if any), or after such time (if any), before the commencement of this Act, and

  (b) records created before such commencement and relating to such particular matters (if any), and

  (c) records created during such period (if any) and relating to such particular matters (if any),

as may be prescribed, after consultation with such Ministers of the Government as the Minister considers appropriate.

(5) Notwithstanding *subsections (1)* and *(4)* but subject to *subsection (6)*, where—

  (a) access to records created before the commencement of this Act is necessary or expedient in order to understand records created after such commencement, or

  (b) records created before such commencement relate to personal information about the person seeking access to them,

subsection (1) shall be construed as conferring the right of access in respect of those records.

(6) *Subsection (5)* shall not be construed as applying, in relation to an individual who is a member of the staff of a public body, the right of access to a record held by a public body that—

  (a) is a personnel record, that is to say, a record relating wholly or mainly to one or more of the following, that is to say, the competence or ability of the individual in his or her capacity as a member of the staff of a public body or his or her employment or employment history or an evaluation of the performance of his or her functions generally or a particular such function as such member,

  (b) was created more than 3 years before the commencement of this Act, and

  (c) is not being used or proposed to be used in a manner or for a purpose that affects, or will or may affect, adversely the interests of the person.

(7) Nothing in this section shall be construed as applying the right of access to an exempt record.

(8) Nothing in this Act shall be construed as prohibiting or restricting a public body

from publishing or giving access to a record (including an exempt record) otherwise than under this Act where such publication or giving of access is not prohibited by law.

(9) A record in the possession of a person who is or was providing a service for a public body under a contract for services shall, if and in so far as it relates to the service, be deemed for the purposes of this Act to be held by the body, and there shall be deemed to be included in the contract a provision that the person shall, if so requested by the body for the purposes of this Act, give the record to the body for retention by it for such period as is reasonable in the particular circumstances.

(10) Where a request under *section 7* would fall to be granted by virtue of *subsection (9)* but for the fact that it relates to a record that contains, with the matter relating to the service concerned, other matter, the head of the public body concerned shall, if it is practicable to do so, prepare a copy, in such form as he or she considers appropriate of so much of the record as does not consist of the other matter aforesaid and the request shall be granted by offering the requester access to the copy.

7.—(1) A person who wishes to exercise the right of access shall make a request, in writing or in such other form as may be determined, addressed to the head of the public body concerned for access to the record concerned— *Request for access to records.*
    (*a*) stating that the request is made under this Act,
    (*b*) containing sufficient particulars in relation to the information concerned to enable the record to be identified by the taking of reasonable steps, and
    (*c*) if the person requires such access to be given in a particular form or manner (being a form or manner referred to in *section 12*), specifying the form or manner of access.

(2) The head shall cause the receipt by him or her of a request under *subsection (1)* to be notified, in writing or in such other form as may be determined, to the requester concerned as soon as may be but not later than 2 weeks after such receipt, and the notification shall include a summary of the provisions of *section 41* and particulars of the rights of review under this Act, the procedure governing the exercise of those rights, and the time limits governing such exercise, in a case to which that section applies.

(3) Where a request under this section is received by the head of a public body ("the head") and the record or records concerned is or are not held by the body ("the first-mentioned body") but, to the knowledge of the head, is or are held by one or more other public bodies, the head shall, as soon as may be, but not more than 2 weeks, after the receipt of the request, cause a copy of the request to be given to the head of the other body or, as the case may be, to the head of that one of the other bodies—
    (*a*) whose functions are, in the opinion of the head, most closely related to the subject matter of the record or records, or
    (*b*) that, in the opinion of the head, is otherwise most appropriate,
and inform the requester concerned, by notice in writing or in such other form as may be determined, of his or her having done so and thereupon—
    (i) the head to whom the copy aforesaid is furnished shall be deemed, for the purposes of this Act, to have received the request under this section and to have received it at the time of the receipt by him or her of the copy, and
    (ii) the head shall be deemed, for the purposes of this Act, not to have received the request.

(4) Where a request under this section relating to more than one record is received by the head of a public body ("the first-mentioned body") and one or more than one (but not all) of the records concerned is or are held by the body, the head shall inform the requester concerned, by notice in writing or in such other form as may be determined, of the names of any other public body that, to his or her knowledge, holds any of the records.

(5) The Minister shall, after consultation with the Commissioner, draw up and publish to heads guidelines for the purposes of *subsection (3)* and *(4)* and heads shall have regard to any such guidelines.

(6) A person shall be deemed to have the knowledge referred to in *subsection (3)* and

(4) if, by the taking of reasonable steps, he or she could obtain that knowledge.

(7) Where—

    (a) a person makes a request for information, or a request for access to a record, to a public body or to a head or a director, or member of the staff, of a public body, other than under and in accordance with this Act, and

    (b) it is not or may not be possible to give the information, or make available the record, other than pursuant to a request in relation to it under and in accordance with *section 7,*

the head shall, if appropriate, cause the person to be informed of the right of access and shall assist, or offer to assist, the person in the preparation of such a request.

Decisions on requests under section 7 and notification of decisions.

8.—(1) Subject to the provisions of this Act, a head shall, as soon as may be, but not later than 4 weeks, after the receipt of a request under *section 7*—

    (a) decide whether to grant or refuse to grant the request or to grant it in part,

    (b) if he or she decides to grant the request, whether wholly or in part, determine the form and manner in which the right of access will be exercised, and

    (c) cause notice, in writing or in such other form as may be determined, of the decision and determination to be given to the requester concerned.

(2) A notice under *subsection (1)* shall specify—

    (a) the decision under that subsection concerned and the day on which it was made,

    (b) unless the head concerned reasonably believes that their disclosure could prejudice the safety or well-being of the person concerned, the name and designation of the person in the public body concerned who is dealing with the request,

    (c) if the request aforesaid is granted, whether wholly or in part—

      (i) the day on which, and the form and manner in which, access to the record concerned will be offered to the requester concerned and the period during which the record will be kept available for the purpose of such access, and

      (ii) the amount of any fee under *section 47* payable by the requester in respect of the grant of the request,

    (d) if the request aforesaid is refused, whether wholly or in part—

      (i) the reasons for the refusal, and

      (ii) unless the refusal is pursuant to *section 19 (5), 22 (2), 23 (2)* or *24 (3),* any provision of this Act pursuant to which the request is refused and the findings on any material issues relevant to the decision and particulars of any matter relating to the public interest taken into consideration for the purposes of the decision,

    (e) if the giving of access to the record is deferred under *section 11,* the reasons for the deferral and the period of the deferral, and

    (f) particulars of rights of review and appeal under this Act in relation to the decision under *subsection (1)* and any other decision referred to in the notice, the procedure governing the exercise of those rights and the time limits governing such exercise.

(3) Subject to the provisions of this Act, where a request is granted under *subsection (1)*—

    (a) if—

      (i) a fee is not charged under *section 47* in respect of the matter,

      (ii) a deposit under that section has been paid and a fee under that section is charged and the amount of the deposit equals or exceeds the amount of the fee, or

      (iii) such a deposit has been paid but such a fee is not charged,

    access to the record concerned shall be offered to the requester concerned forthwith and the record shall be kept available for the purpose of such access for a period of 4 weeks thereafter, and (*b*) if a fee is so charged, access to the record concerned shall be offered to the requester concerned as soon as may be, but not more than one week, after the day on which the fee is received by the public body concerned, and the record shall be kept available for the purpose of such access until—

(*i*)   the expiration of the period of 4 weeks from such receipt, or

(*ii*) the expiration of the period of 8 weeks from the receipt by the requester concerned of the notice under *subsection (1)* concerned,

whichever is the earlier.

(4) In deciding whether to grant or refuse to grant a request under *section 7*—

(*a*) any reason that the requester gives for the request, and

(*b*) any belief or opinion of the head as to what are the reasons of the requester for the request,

shall be disregarded.

(5) This section shall not be construed as requiring the inclusion in a notice under *subsection (1)* of matter that, if it were included in a record, would cause the record to be an exempt record.

(6) References in this section to the grant of a request under *section 7* include references to such a grant pursuant to *section 13*.

9.—(1) The head may, as respects a request under *section 7* received by him or her ("the specified request"), extend the period specified in *section 8 (1)* for consideration of the request by such period as he or she considers necessary but not exceeding a period of 4 weeks if in the opinion of the head— *Extension of time for consideration of requests under section 7.*

(*a*) the request relates to such number of records, or

(*b*) the number of other requests under *section 7* relating either to the record or records to which the specified request relates or to information corresponding to that to which the specified request relates or to both that have been made to the public body concerned before the specified request was made to it and in relation to which a decision under *section 8* has not been made is such,

that compliance with that subsection within the period specified therein is not reasonably possible.

(2) Where a period is extended under this section, the head concerned shall cause notice in writing or in such other form as may be determined, to be given to the requester concerned, before the expiration of the period, of the extension and the period thereof and reasons therefor.

(3) The reference in *section 8 (1)* to 4 weeks shall be construed in accordance with any extension under this section of that period.

10.—(1) A head to whom a request under *section 7* is made may refuse to grant the request if— *Refusal on administrative grounds to grant requests under section 7.*

(*a*) the record concerned does not exist or cannot be found after all reasonable steps to ascertain its whereabouts have been taken,

(*b*) the request does not comply with *section 7 (1) (b)*,

(*c*) in the opinion of the head, granting the request would, by reason of the number or nature of the records concerned or the nature of the information concerned, require the retrieval and examination of such number of records or an examination of such kind of the records concerned as to cause a substantial and unreasonable interference with or disruption of the other work of the public body concerned,

(*d*) publication of the record is required by law and is intended to be effected not later than 12 weeks after the receipt of the request by the head,

(*e*) the request is, in the opinion of the head, frivolous or vexatious, or

(*f*) a fee or deposit payable under *section 47* has not been paid.

(2) A head shall not refuse, pursuant to *paragraph (b)* or *(c)* of *subsection (1)*, to grant a request under *section 7* unless he or she has assisted, or offered to assist, the requester

concerned in an endeavour so to amend the request that it no longer falls within that paragraph.

Deferral of
access to
records.
11.—(1) Where a request is made under *section 7*, and—

    (*a*) the record concerned was prepared solely for the information of either or both of the Houses of the Oireachtas or a committee of either or both of such Houses and copies of the record are intended to be laid before either or both of such Houses or given to such a committee or otherwise published to members of either or both of such Houses or such a committee on a day failing within a reasonable period after the receipt by the head concerned of the request ("the specified day"), or

    (*b*) information contained in the record concerned falls within *paragraph (b)*, *(d)* or *(e)* of *section 20 (2)* and the giving of access to the record on or before a particular day ("the specified day") would, in the opinion of the head concerned be contrary to the public interest, or

    (*c*) the record concerned is held by a public body, being a Department of State or the Office of the Tánaiste and the Minister of the Government in whom functions in relation to the public body are vested considers that the record or part thereof or any matter to which it relates is of such interest to the public generally that he or she intends to inform either or both of the Houses of the Oireachtas of the contents of the record or part or of the matter or otherwise to publish the contents of the record or part or information relating to the matter on a day not later than one week after the appropriate time specified in *section 8 (3)* ("the specified day"),

the head concerned may defer the offering of access to the record to the requester concerned until the day immediately after the specified day.

(2) *Section 8 (3)* shall be construed and have effect in relation to a case in which the offering of access to a record is deferred under this section as if—

    (*a*) *paragraph (a)* thereof required access to the record to be offered to the requester concerned forthwith upon the expiration of the period of the deferral and the record to be kept available for the purpose of such access for a period of 4 weeks thereafter, and

    (*b*) *paragraph (b)* thereof required access to the record to be offered to the requester as soon as may be, but not more than one week, after—

        (i) the expiration of the period of the deferral, or

        (ii) the day on which the fee under *section 47* concerned is received by the public body concerned,

      whichever is the later and the record to be kept available for the purpose of such access until—

        (I) the expiration of the period of 4 weeks from such receipt, or

        (II) the expiration of the period of 4 weeks from the expiration of the period of the deferral, whichever is the later.

Manner of
access to
records.
12.—(1) A head may give access under this Act to a record by providing the requester with—

    (*a*) a copy of the record,

    (*b*) a transcript of the information concerned,

    (*c*) a computer disk or other electronic device containing the information,

    (*d*) a reasonable opportunity to inspect the record,

    (*e*) in case the record is of sound or visual images, a reasonable opportunity to hear or view the record,

    (*f*) in case the information is in shorthand or other code, the information in decodified form and in written form or such other form as may be determined,

    (*g*) the information in such other form or manner as may be determined, or

    (*h*) the information in a combination of any two or more of the foregoing.

(2) Where a head decides to grant a request under *section 7* and the request is for access in a particular form or manner to a record, such access shall be given in that form or manner unless the head concerned is satisfied—

    (*a*) that such access in another form or manner specified in or determined under *subsection (1)* would be significantly more efficient, or

    (*b*) that the giving of access in the form or manner requested would—

        (i)   be physically detrimental to the record,

        (ii) involve an infringement of copyright (other than copyright owned by the State, the Government or the public body concerned),

        (iii) conflict with a legal duty or obligation of a public body, or

        (iv) prejudice, impair or damage any interest protected by *Part III* or *section 46*.

(3) Where a head decides to grant a request under *section 7* but not to give access to the record concerned in the form or manner specified in the request, he or she shall give such access—

    (*a*) if the case is one to which *paragraph (a)* of *subsection (2)* applies, in the appropriate form or manner having regard to that paragraph, and

    (*b*) if the case is one to which *paragraph (b)* of that subsection applies, in such other form or manner specified in or determined under *subsection (1)* as may be agreed by the head and the requester or, if those persons are unable to agree upon such a form, in such form specified in *subsection (1)* as the head considers appropriate.

13.—(1) Where a request under *section 7* would fall to be granted but for the fact that it relates to a record that is an exempt record, by reason of the inclusion in it, with other matter, of particular matter, the head of the public body concerned, shall, if it is practicable to do so, prepare a copy, in such form as he or she considers appropriate, of so much of the record as does not consist of the particular matter aforesaid and the request shall be granted by offering the requester access to the copy.   *Access to parts of records.*

(2) *Subsection* (1) shall not apply in relation to a record if the copy provided for thereby would be misleading.

(3) Where a requester is offered access to a copy of part of a record under this section, then (unless the record is one to which *section 19 (5)*, *22 (2)*, *23 (2)* or *24 (3)* applies), the notice under *section 8 (1)* concerned shall specify that such access is offered pursuant to this section and that the copy does not purport to be a copy of the complete record to which the request under *section 7* relates and shall also specify the nature of the matter contained in the record by virtue of which *subsection (1)* applies to the record.

14.—(1) This section applies to a decision made pursuant to this Act by a person to whom the function concerned stood delegated at the time of the making of the decision, being—   *Review by heads of decision.*

    (*a*) a decision to refuse to grant a request under *section 7*, whether wholly or in part, (other than a request to which *section 29* applies) ("a request") in relation to the record concerned,

    (*b*) a decision under *section 11* to defer the offering of access to a record falling within *paragraph (a)* of *subsection (1)* of that section,

    (*c*) a decision under *section 12* to grant a request by giving access to the record concerned in a form other than that specified in the request,

    (*d*) a decision under *section 13* to grant a request under *section 7* by offering the requester concerned access to a copy of part only of the record concerned,

    (*e*) a decision under *section 17* to refuse to amend a record,

    (*f*) a decision under *section 18* in relation to the contents of a statement furnished under *subsection (1)* of that section or to refuse an application under that subsection, or (*g*) a decision to charge a fee or deposit, or a fee or deposit of a particular amount, under *section 47.*

(2) Subject to the provisions of this section, the head of the public body concerned, on application to him or her in that behalf, in writing or in such other form as may be determined, by a relevant person—

    (*a*) may review a decision to which this section applies, and

    (*b*) following the review, may, as he or she considers appropriate—

        (i) affirm or vary the decision, or

        (ii) annul the decision and, if appropriate, make such decision in relation to the matter as he or she considers proper,

in accordance with this Act.

(3) A person to whom a function under this section stands delegated under *section 4* shall not perform that function in relation to a decision to which this section applies that was made by a member of the staff of the public body concerned whose rank is the same as or higher than that of the person aforesaid.

(4) A decision under *subsection (2)* shall be made, and the head concerned shall cause notice thereof, in writing or in such other form as may be determined, to be given to the relevant person and any other person whom he or she considers should be notified thereof, not later than 3 weeks after the receipt by the head of the application for the review under that subsection concerned.

(5) A notice under *subsection (4)* shall specify—

    (*a*) the day on which the decision concerned under that subsection was made,

    (*b*) if the decision is to grant, in whole or in part, the request under *section 7* concerned, the information referred to in *section 8 (2) (c)*,

    (*c*) if the decision is to refuse to grant, wholly or in part, the request aforesaid, the information specified in *subparagraph (i)* of *paragraph (d)* of *section 8 (2)* and, if the refusal is not pursuant to *section 10 (1) (c), 19 (5), 22 (2), 23 (2),* or *24 (3),* the information specified in *subparagraph (ii)* of that paragraph,

    (*d*) if the decision is to defer the giving of access to the record concerned, the reasons for the deferral and the period of the deferral,

    (*e*) if the decision is a decision referred to in *paragraph (c), (d), (e), (f)* or *(g)* of *subsection (1),* the reasons for the decision, and

    (*f*) particulars of he rights of review and appeal under this Act in relation to the decision, the procedure governing the exercise of those rights and the time limits governing such exercise.

(6) This section shall not be construed as requiring the inclusion in a notice under *subsection (4)* of matter that, if it were included in a record, would cause the record to be an exempt record.

(7) An application under *subsection (2)* shall be made not later than 4 weeks after the notification under this Act of the decision concerned to the relevant person concerned or, in a case in which the head concerned is of the opinion that there are reasonable grounds for extending that period, the expiration of such longer period as he or she may determine.

(8) The relevant person concerned may, at any time before the making of a decision under *subsection (2)* following the review concerned, by notice in writing or in such other form as may be determined, given to the head concerned, withdraw the application concerned under that subsection.

(9) *Subsection (3)* of *section 8* shall apply in relation to a case where a decision under *subsection (2)* is to grant a request under *section 7* or to annul or vary a deferral under *section 11* with the modification that the reference in the said *subsection (3)* to the grant of a request under *subsection (1)* of *section 8* shall be construed as a reference to the making of the decision under *subsection (2).*

(10) Subject to the provisions of this Act, a decision under *subsection (2)* shall—

    (*a*) in so far as it is inconsistent with the decision to which this section applies concerned, have effect in lieu thereof, and

    (*b*) be binding on the parties concerned.

(11) In this section "relevant person", in relation to a decision to which this section applies, means—
- (*a*) the requester concerned, or
- (*b*) if the decision is under *section 17 or 18*, the person who made the application concerned.

15.—(1) A public body shall cause to be prepared and published and to be made available in accordance with *subsection (7)* a reference book containing— Publication of information about public bodies.
- (*a*) a general description of its structure and organisation, functions, powers and duties, any services it provides for the public and the procedures by which any such services may be availed of by the public,
- (*b*) a general description of the classes of records held by it, giving such particulars as are reasonably necessary to facilitate the exercise of the right of access,
- (*c*) a general description of the matters referred to in *paragraphs (a)* and *(b)* of *section 16 (1)*,
- (*d*) the arrangements made by the body—
  - (i) to enable a person to obtain access to records held by the body,
  - (ii) to enable an individual to apply for the amendment of any such records that relate to personal information in respect of the individual, and
  - (iii) to enable a person to whom *section 18 (1)* applies to obtain the information specified therein,
- (*e*) the names and designations of the members of the staff of the body responsible for carrying out the arrangements aforesaid (unless the head of the body reasonably believes that publication of that information could threaten the physical safety or well-being of the persons),
- (*f*) the address or addresses at which requests under *section 7* or applications under *section 17 or 18* should be given,
- (*g*) appropriate information concerning—
  - (i) any rights of review or appeal in respect of decisions made by the body (including rights of review and appeal under this Act), and
  - (ii) the procedure governing the exercise of those rights and any time limits governing such exercise,
- (*h*) any other information that the head of the body considers relevant for the purpose of facilitating the exercise of the right of access, and
- (*i*) information in relation to such other matters (if any) as may be prescribed.

(2) A reference book prepared under *subsection (1)* shall be made available in accordance with *subsection (7)*—
- (*a*) in case the body concerned is a body specified in *paragraph 1* (other than *subparagraph (3), (4)* and *(5)*) of the *First Schedule*, upon the commencement of this Act,
- (*b*) in case the body is a local authority, upon the commencement of the said *subparagraph (3)*,
- (*c*) in case the body is a health board, upon the commencement of the said *subparagraph (4)*, and
- (*d*) in case the body is a body standing prescribed under *section 3* for the purposes of the said *subparagraph (5)*, upon such prescription,

and thereafter a version, appropriately revised, of the book shall be prepared and published and shall be made available as aforesaid by the body not less frequently than 3 years after the latest such book was so made available by the body and as soon as may be after any significant alterations or additions fall to be made in or to the latest such book so made available.

(3) In preparing a reference book under *subsection (1)*, a public body shall have regard to the fact that the purpose of the book is to assist members of the public in ascertaining and exercising their rights under this Act.

(4) At the time of the publication of a reference book under *subsection (1)* or *(2)*, the

body concerned shall furnish to the Minister a summary thereof and the Minister shall cause the summaries furnished to him or her under this subsection to be collated and shall cause a reference book containing the summaries as so collated to be published and to be made available in accordance with *subsection (7)* not later than 15 months after the commencement of this Act and thereafter not less frequently than 3 years after the latest such book is published and so made available and as soon as may be after any significant alterations or additions fall to be made in or to the latest such book so made available.

(5) The Minister shall ensure that appropriate measures are taken by public bodies, as respects training of staff, organisational arrangements and such other matters as the Minister considers appropriate, for the purpose of facilitating compliance by the bodies with this Act and, without prejudice to the generality of *paragraph (b)* of *section 3 (1)*, may, by regulations made under that paragraph after consultation with the Commissioner and the Director of the National Archives (within the meaning of the National Archives Act, 1986), make provision for the management and maintenance of records held by public bodies.

(6) (*a*) As soon as may be after the end of a period specified in *paragraph (d)*, the Minister shall prepare a report in writing of the measures taken by public bodies pursuant to *subsection (5)* during that period.

(*b*) A report under this subsection shall include a report of any measures taken by a public body during the period to which the report relates consequent upon a report under *section 36 (4)*.

(*c*) The Minister. shall cause a copy of a report under this subsection to be furnished as soon as may be to the committee (within the meaning of *section 32*).

(*d*) The periods referred to in *paragraph (a)* are:

    (*i*)   the period of 3 months beginning on the commencement of this Act, and

    (*ii*) the period of 12 months beginning on the expiration of the period aforesaid and each subsequent period of 12 months beginning on the expiration of the period of 12 months immediately preceding.

(7) A book referred to in *subsection (1), (2)* or *(4)* shall be made available for inspection free of charge, and for removal free of charge or, at the discretion of the head concerned or the Minister, as may be appropriate, for purchase, at such places as the head or, as may be appropriate, the Minister may determine and the head or the Minister, as may be appropriate, shall cause notice of those places to be published in such manner as he or she considers adequate for the purposes of this section and, if the book relates to a local authority or a health board, a copy of it shall be given to each member of the authority or board.

(8) *Subsection (1)* does not apply to any matter by reason of which a record in which it is included is an exempt record.

Publication of information regarding rules and practices in relation to certain decisions by public bodies.

16.—(1) A public body shall cause to be prepared and published and to be made available in accordance with *subsection (5)*—

(*a*) the rules, procedures, practices, guidelines and interpretations used by the body, and an index of any precedents kept by the body, for the purposes of decisions, determinations or recommendations, under or for the purposes of any enactment or scheme administered by the body with respect to rights, privileges, benefits, obligations, penalties or other sanctions to which members of the public are or may be entitled or subject under the enactment or scheme, and

(*b*) appropriate information in relation to the manner or intended manner of administration of any such enactment or scheme.

(2) A publication prepared under *subsection (1)* shall be made available in accordance with *subsection (5)*—

(*a*) in case the body concerned is a body specified in *paragraph 1* (other than *subparagraph (3), (4)* or *(5)*) of the *First Schedule*, upon the commencement of this Act,

(*b*) in case the body is a local authority, upon the commencement of the said *subparagraph (3)*, (*c*) in case the body is a health board, upon the commencement of the said *subparagraph (4)*, and

(*d*) in case the body is a body standing prescribed under *section 3* for the purposes of the said *subparagraph (5)*, upon such prescription,

and thereafter a version, appropriately revised, of the publication shall be prepared and published and shall be made available as aforesaid by the body not less frequently than 3 years after the latest such publication was so made available by the body and as soon as may be after any significant alterations or additions fall to be made in or to the latest such publication so made available.

(3) If the material specified in *paragraph (a)* of *subsection (1)* is not published and made available in accordance with this section or the material so published and purporting to be the material aforesaid is incomplete or inaccurate and a person shows—

(*a*) that he or she was not aware of a rule, procedure, practice, guideline, interpretation or precedent referred to in *subsection (1) (a)* ("the rule") or of a particular requirement of the rule, and

(*b*) that, but for such non-publication, non-availability, incompleteness or incorrectness, as the case may be, he or she would have been so aware,

the public body concerned shall, if and in so far as it is practicable to do so, ensure that the person is not subjected to any prejudice (not being a penalty imposed by a court upon conviction of an offence) by reason only of the application of the rule or requirement if the person could lawfully have avoided that prejudice if he or she had been aware of the rule or requirement.

(4) *Subsection (3)* shall not apply in a case where the public body concerned shows that reasonable steps were taken by it to bring the rule or requirement concerned to the notice of those affected by it.

(5) A publication referred to in *subsection (1)* or *(2)* shall be made available for inspection free of charge, and for removal free of charge or, at the discretion of the head concerned, for purchase, at such places as the head concerned may determine and the head shall cause notice of those places to be published in such manner as he or she considers adequate for the purposes of this section and if the publication relates to a local authority or a health board, a copy of it shall be given to each member of the authority or board.

(6) A precedent referred to in an index specified in *subsection (1)* shall, on request therefor to the public body concerned, be made available to the person concerned in accordance with *subsection (5)*.

(7) *Subsection (1)* does not apply to any matter by reason of which a record in which it is included is an exempt record.

17.—(1) Where personal information in a record held by a public body is incomplete, incorrect or misleading, the head of the body shall, on application to him or her in that behalf, in writing or in such other form as may be determined, by the individual to whom the information relates, amend the record— *Amendment of records relating to personal information.*

(i) by altering it so as to make the information complete or correct or not misleading, as may be appropriate,

(ii) by adding to the record a statement specifying the respects in which the body is satisfied that the information is incomplete, incorrect or misleading, as may he appropriate, or

(iii) by deleting the information from it.

(2) An application under *subsection (1)* shall in so far as is practicable—

(*a*) specify the record concerned and the amendment required, and

(*b*) include appropriate information in support of the application.

(3) The head concerned shall, as soon as may be, but not later than 4 weeks, after the receipt by him or her of an application under *subsection (1)*, decide whether to grant or refuse to grant the application and shall cause notice, in writing or in such other form as may be determined, of his or her decision and, if the decision is to grant it, of the manner of such grant to be given to the person concerned.

(4) (*a*) If the grant of an application under *subsection (1)* is refused, the head concerned shall—

    (i)   attach to the record concerned the application or a copy of it or, if that is not practicable, a notation indicating that the application has been made, and

    (ii)   include in the notification under *subsection (3)* particulars of—

        (I)   rights of review and appeal under this Act in relation to the decision to refuse to grant the application, and

        (II) the procedure governing the exercise of those rights and any time limits governing such exercise.

(*b*) *Paragraph (a)(i)* does not apply in relation to a case in which the head concerned is of opinion that the application concerned is defamatory or the alterations or additions to which it relates to the record concerned would be unnecessarily voluminous.

(5) Where a record is amended pursuant to this section, the public body concerned shall take all reasonable steps to notify of the amendment—

    (*a*) any person to whom access to the record was granted under this Act, and

    (*b*) any other public body to whom a copy of the record was given,

during the period of one year ending on the date on which the amendment was effected.

Right of person to information regarding acts of public bodies affecting the person.

18.—(1) The head of a public body shall, on application to him or her in that behalf, in writing or in such other form as may be determined, by a person who is affected by an act of the body and has a material interest in a matter affected by the act or to which it relates, not later than 4 weeks after the receipt of the application, cause a statement, in writing or in such other form as may be determined, to be given to the person—

    (*a*) of the reasons for the act, and

    (*b*) of any findings on any material issues of fact made for the purposes of the act.

(2) Nothing in this section shall be construed as requiring—

    (*a*) the giving to a person of information contained in an exempt record, or

    (*b*) the disclosure of the existence or non-existence of a record if the non-disclosure of its existence or non-existence is required by this Act.

(3) *Subsection (1)* shall not apply to—

    (*a*) a decision of the Civil Service Commissioners pursuant to subparagraph (d) or (e) of section 17 (1) of the Civil Service Commissioners Act, 1956, not to accept a person as qualified for a position referred to in that section, or

    (b) a decision of the Local Appointments Commissioners made by virtue of section 7 (3) of the Local Authorities (Officers and Employees) Act, 1926, not to recommend a person to a local authority for appointment to an office referred to in that section,

if, in the opinion of the head concerned, the giving of a statement under *subsection (1)* in relation to the decision would be likely to prejudice the effectiveness of the process for selecting a person for appointment to the position or office.

(4) If, pursuant to *subsection (2)* or (*3*), the head of a public body decides not to cause a statement to be given under *subsection (1)* to a person, the head shall, not later than 4 weeks after the receipt of the application concerned under *subsection (1)*, cause notice, in writing or in such other form as may be determined, of the decision to be given to the person.

(5) For the purposes of this section a person has a material interest in a matter affected by an act of a public body or to which such an act relates if the consequence or effect of the act may be to confer on or withhold from the person a benefit without also conferring it on or withholding it from persons in general or a class of persons which is of significant size having regard to all the circumstances and of which the person is a member.

(6) In this section—

"act", in relation to a public body, includes a decision (other than a decision under this Act) of the body;

"benefit", in relation to a person, includes—
    (*a*) any advantage to the person,
    (*b*) in respect of an act of a public body done at the request of the person, any consequence or effect thereof relating to the person, and
    (*c*) the avoidance of a loss, liability, penalty, forfeiture, punishment or other disadvantage affecting the person.

PART III

EXEMPT RECORDS

19.—(1) A head may refuse to grant a request under *section 7* if the record concerned— [Meetings of the Government.]
    (*a*) has been, or is proposed to be, submitted to the Government for their consideration by a Minister of the Government or the Attorney General and was created for that purpose,
    (*b*) is a record of the Government other than a record by which a decision of the Government is published to the general public by or on behalf of the Government, or
    (*c*) contains information (including advice) for a member of the Government, the Attorney General, a Minister of State, the Secretary to the Government or the Assistant Secretary to the Government for use by him or her solely for the purpose of the transaction of any business of the Government at a meeting of the Government.

(2) A head shall refuse to grant a request under *section 7* if the record concerned—
    (*a*) contains the whole or part of a statement made at a meeting of the Government or information that reveals, or from which may be inferred, the substance of the whole or part of such a statement, and
    (*b*) is not a record—
        (i) referred to in *paragraph (a)* or *(c)* of *subsection (1)*, or
        (ii) by which a decision of the Government is published to the general public by or on behalf of the Government.

(3) Subject to the provisions of this Act, *subsection (1)* does not apply to a record referred to in that subsection—
    (*a*) if and in so far as it contains factual information relating to a decision of the Government that has been published to the general public, or
    (*b*) if the record relates to a decision of the Government that was made more than 5 years before the receipt by the head concerned of the request under *section 7* concerned.

(4) A decision to grant a request under *section 7* in respect of a record to which *paragraph (a)* or *(b)* of *subsection (1)* applies shall not be made unless, in so far as it is practicable to do so, the head concerned has, prior to the making of the decision, consulted in relation to the request with—
    (*a*) the leader of each political party to which belonged a member of the Government that made any decision to which the record relates, and
    (*b*) any member of the Government aforesaid who was not a member of a political party.

(5) Where a request under *section 7* relates to a record to which *subsection (1)* applies, or would, if the record existed, apply, and the head concerned is satisfied that the disclosure of the existence or non-existence of the record would be contrary to the public interest, he or she shall refuse to grant the request and shall not disclose to the requester concerned whether or not the record exists.

(6) In this section—

"decision of the Government" includes the noting or approving by the Government of a record submitted to them;

"record" includes a preliminary or other draft of the whole or part of the material contained in the record;

"Government" includes a committee of the Government, that is to say, a committee appointed by the Government whose membership consists of—
    (*a*) members of the Government, or
    (*b*) one or more members of the Government together with either or both of the following:
        (i)   one or more Ministers of State,
        (ii) the Attorney General

Deliberations of public bodies.

20.—(1) A head may refuse to grant a request under *section 7*—
    (*a*) if the record concerned contains matter relating to the deliberative processes of the public body concerned (including opinions, advice, recommendations, and the results of consultations, considered by the body, the head of the body, or a member of the body or of the staff of the body for the purpose of those processes), and
    (*b*) the granting of the request would, in the opinion of the head, be contrary to the public interest,
and, without prejudice to the generality of *paragraph* (*b*), the head shall, in determining whether to grant or refuse to grant the request, consider whether the grant thereof would be contrary to the public interest by reason of the fact that the requester concerned would thereby become aware of a significant decision that the body proposes to make.

(2) *Subsection (1)* does not apply to a record if and in so far as it contains—
    (*a*) matter used, or intended to be used, by a public body for the purpose of making decisions, determinations or recommendations referred to in *section 16*,
    (*b*) factual (including statistical) information and analyses thereof,
    (*c*) the reasons for the making of a decision by a public body,
    (*d*) a report of an investigation or analysis of the performance, efficiency or effectiveness of a public body in relation to the functions generally or a particular function of the body,
    (*e*) a report, study or analysis of a scientific or technical expert relating to the subject of his or her expertise or a report containing opinions or advice of such an expert and not being a report used or commissioned for the purposes of a decision of a public body made pursuant to any enactment or scheme.

Functions and negotiations of public bodies.

21.—(1) A head may refuse to grant a request under *section 7* if access to the record concerned could, in the opinion of the head, reasonably be expected to—
    (*a*) prejudice the effectiveness of tests, examinations, investigations, inquiries or audits conducted by or on behalf of the public body concerned or the procedures or methods employed for the conduct thereof,
    (*b*) have a significant, adverse effect on the performance by the body of any of its functions relating to management (including industrial relations and management of its staff), or
    (*c*) disclose positions taken, or to be taken, or plans, procedures, criteria or instructions used or followed, or to be used or followed, for the purpose of any negotiations carried on or being, or to be, carried on by or on behalf of the Government or a public body.

(2) *Subsection (1)* shall not apply in relation to a case in which in the opinion of the head concerned, the public interest would, on balance, be better served by granting than by refusing to grant the request under *section 7* concerned.

22.—(1) A head shall refuse to grant a request under *section 7* if the record concerned— Parliamentary, court and certain other matters.

    (*a*) would be exempt from production in proceedings in a court on the ground of legal professional privilege,

    (*b*) is such that its disclosure would constitute contempt of court, or

    (*c*) consists of—

        (i)   the private papers of a representative in the European Parliament or a member of a local authority or a health board, or

        (ii) opinions, advice, recommendations, or the results of consultations, considered by—

            (I) either House of the Oireachtas or the Chairman or Deputy Chairman or any other member of either such House or a member of the staff of the Office of the Houses of the Oireachtas for the purposes of the proceedings at a sitting of either such House, or

            (II) a committee appointed by either such House or jointly by both such Houses and consisting of members of either or both of such Houses or a member of such a committee or a member of the staff of the Office of the blouses of the Oireachtas tin the purposes of the proceedings at a meeting of such a committee.

(2)Where a request under *section 7* relates to a record to which *subsection (1)(a)* applies, or would, if the record existed, apply, and the head concerned is satisfied that the disclosure of the existence or non-existence of the record would be contrary to the public interest, he or she shall refuse to grant the request and shall not disclose to the requester concerned whether or not the record exists.

23.—(1) A head may refuse to grant a request under *section 7* if access to the record concerned could, in the opinion of the head, reasonably be expected to— Law enforcement and public safety.

    (*a*) prejudice or impair—

        (i)   the prevention, detection or investigation of offences, the apprehension or prosecution of offenders or the effectiveness of lawful methods, systems, plans or procedures employed for the purposes of the matters aforesaid,

        (ii)   the enforcement of, compliance with or administration of any law,

        (iii) lawful methods, systems, plans or procedures for ensuring the safety of the public and the safety or security of persons and property,

        (iv) the fairness of criminal proceedings in a court or of civil proceedings in a court or other tribunal,

        (v)   the security of a penal institution,

        (vi) the security of the Central Mental Hospital,

        (vii) the security of a building or other structure or a vehicle, ship, boat or aircraft,

        (viii) the security of any system of communications, whether internal or external, of the Garda Síochána, the Defence Forces, the Revenue Commissioners or a penal institution,

    (*b*) reveal or lead to the revelation of the identity of a person who has given information to a public body in confidence in relation to the enforcement or administration of the civil law or any other source of such information given in confidence, or

    (*c*) facilitate the commission of an offence.

(2) Where a request under *section 7* relates to a record to which *subsection (1)* applies, or would, if the record existed, apply, and the head concerned is satisfied that the disclosure of the existence or non-existence of the record would have an effect specified in *paragraph (a)*, *(b)* or *(c)* of that subsection, he or she shall refuse to grant the request and shall not disclose to the requester concerned whether or not the record exists.

(3) *Subsection (1)* does not apply to a record—

    (*a*) if it—

(i)   discloses that an investigation for the purpose of the enforcement of any
      law, or anything done in the course of such an investigation or for the
      purposes of the prevention or detection of offences or the apprehen-
      sion or prosecution of offenders, is not authorised by law or contra-
      venes any law. or

(ii) contains information concerning—

      (I) the performance of the functions of a public body whose functions
           include functions relating to the enforcement of law or the en-
           suring of the safety of the public (including the effectiveness
           and efficiency of such performance), or

      (II) the merits or otherwise or the success or otherwise of any pro-
           gramme, scheme or policy of a public body for preventing, de-
           tecting or investigating contraventions of the law or the effec-
           tiveness or efficiency of the implementation of any such pro-
           gramme, scheme or policy by a public body,

and

(b) in the opinion of the head concerned, the public interest would, on balance, be
     better served by granting than by refusing to grant the request concerned.

(4) In *subsection (1)* "penal institution" means—

(a) a place to which the Prisons Acts, 1826 to 1980, apply,

(b) a military prison or detention barrack within the meaning, in each case, of the
     Defence Act, 1954,

(c) Saint Patrick's Institution, or

(d) an institution established under the Children Act, 1908, in which young offend-
     ers are detained.

24.—(1) A head may refuse to grant a request under *section 7* in relation to a record
(and, in particular, but without prejudice to the generality otherwise of this subsection, to a
record to which *subsection (2)* applies) if, in the opinion of the head, access to it could
reasonably be expected to affect adversely—

(a) the security of the State,

(b) the defence of the State,

(c) the international relations of the State, or

(d) matters relating to Northern Ireland.

(2) This subsection applies to a record that—

(a) contains information—

     (i)   that was obtained or prepared for the purpose of intelligence in respect
           of the security or defence of the State, or

     (ii) that relates to—

           (I) the tactics, strategy or operations of the Defence Forces in or out-
                side the State, or

           (II) the detection, prevention, or suppression of activities calculated or
                tending to undermine the public order or the authority of the
                State (which expression has the same meaning as in *section 2* of
                the Offences against the State Act, 1939),

(b) contains a communication between a Minister of the Government and a diplo-
     matic mission or consular post in the State or a communication between the
     Government or a person acting on behalf of the Government and another
     government or a person acting on behalf of another government,

(c) contains a communication between a Minister of the Government and a diplo-
     matic mission or consular post of the State,

(d) contains information communicated in confidence to any person in or outside
     the State from any person in or outside the State and relating to a matter
     referred to in *subsection (1)* or to the protection of human rights and ex-
     pressed by the latter person to be confidential or to be communicated in con-

fidence,

(*e*) contains information communicated in confidence from, to or within an international organisation of states or a subsidiary organ of such an organisation or an institution or body of the European Union or relates to negotiations between the State and such an organisation, organ, institution or body or within or in relation to such an organisation, organ, institution or body, or

(*f*) is a record of an organisation, organ, institution or body referred to in *paragraph (e)* containing information the disclosure of which is prohibited by the organisation, organ, institution or body.

(3) Where a request under *section 7* relates to a record to which *subsection (1)* applies, or would, if the record, existed, apply, and the head concerned is satisfied that the disclosure of the existence or non-existence of the record would prejudice a matter referred to in that subsection, he or she shall refuse to grant the request and shall not disclose to the requester concerned whether or not the record exits.

25.—(1) (*a*) Subject to *paragraph (b)*, where—

   (i) a Minister of the Government or the head of a public body (other than a Department of State or the Office of the Tánaiste) in relation to which functions stand conferred on that Minister of the Government—

     (I) pursuant to *section 8*, refuses to grant a request to him or her under *section 7*, or

     (II) pursuant to *section 14*, upholds a decision, or decides, to refuse to grant a request under *section 7*,

     because he or she is satisfied that, by virtue of *section 23* or *24*, the record concerned is an exempt record, and

   (ii) the Minister of the Government is satisfied, that the record is of sufficient sensitivity or seriousness to justify his or her doing so, the Minister of the Government may declare, in a certificate issued by him or her ("a certificate"), that the record is, by virtue of *section 23* or *24*, an exempt record.

(*b*) A Minister of the Government shall not issue a certificate in respect of a record the subject of a decision referred to in *clause (I)* or *(II)* of *paragraph (a) (i)* by the head of a public body (other than a Department of State or the Office of the Tánaiste) unless he or she has been requested by the head in writing or such other form as may be determined, to do so.

(2) Where an application is made to a head for the review under *section 14* of a decision to refuse to grant a request under *section 7*, a certificate shall not be issued in respect of the record concerned more than 3 weeks after the date of the receipt of the application by that head.

(3) While a certificate is in force—

(*a*) the record to which it relates shall, subject to the provisions of this Act, be deemed conclusively to be an exempt record, and

(*b*) an application for a review under *section 14* or *34*, as may be appropriate, of the decision concerned under *section 8* or *14* in relation to the record shall not lie.

(4) A document purporting to be a certificate and to be signed by a Minister of the Government shall, unless the contrary is proved, be deemed to be a certificate of that Minister of the Government and to be in force and shall be received in any proceedings in a court or under *section 14* or *34* without further proof.

(5) A certificate shall specify—

(*a*) the request under *section 7* concerned,

(*b*) the provisions of *section 23* or *24*, as may be appropriate, by reference to which the record to which it relates is an exempt record,

(*c*) the date on which the certificate is signed by the Minister of the Government concerned and the date of its expiration, and

(*d*) the name of the requester,

Conclusiveness of ceratin decisions pursuant to sections 23 and 24 and shall be signed by the Minister of the Government by whom it is issued.

(6) Upon the issue of a certificate, the Minister of the Government concerned shall cause—

> (*a*) a copy of the certificate to be furnished forthwith to the requester concerned, and
>
> (*b*) a copy of the certificate and a statement in writing of the reasons why the record to which it relates is an exempt record and of the matter by reference to which the Minister of the Government is satisfied that *subsection (1) (a) (ii)* applies to the record to be furnished forthwith to the Taoiseach and such other Ministers of the Government as may be prescribed.

(7) (*a*) Subject to *paragraph (b)*, the Taoiseach, jointly with any other Ministers of the Government standing prescribed under *subsection (6)*, shall, as soon as may be after the expiration of each period of 6 months (or such other period not exceeding 12 months in length as may be prescribed) beginning with the period from the commencement of this Act, review the operation of *subsection (1)* during that period.

> (*b*) A Minister of the Government shall not take part in a review under this subsection in so far as it relates to a certificate issued by him or her but may make submissions to the other Ministers of the Government concerned in relation to the part of such a review in which he or she is precluded as aforesaid from taking part.
>
> (*c*) If, following a review under this subsection, the Ministers of the Government concerned are not satisfied—
>
>> (i)   that a record to which the certificate concerned relates is an exempt record, or
>>
>> (ii) that any of the information contained in the record is of sufficient sensitivity or seriousness to justify the continuance in force of the certificate,
>
> they shall request the Minister of the Government concerned to revoke the certificate.
>
> (*d*) A Minister of the Government may, for the purposes of a review by that Minister of the Government under this subsection, examine all relevant records held by or on behalf of or under the control of another head.

(8) (*a*) The Taoiseach may, at any time, review the operation of *subsection (1)* in so far as it relates to any other Minister of the Government or the issue of a particular certificate by another Minister of the Government.

> (*b*) *Paragraphs (c)* and *(d)* of *subsection (7)* shall have effect in relation to a review under this subsection with the necessary modifications.

(9) A Minister of the Government may, and shall, if so requested pursuant to *subsection (7) (c)*, by instrument signed by him or her, revoke a certificate issued by that Minister of the Government and, if he or she does so, he or she shall cause the requester concerned to be furnished forthwith with a copy of the instrument.

(10) If a certificate or the decision concerned under *section 8* or *14* in relation to a record to which a certificate relates is annulled by the High Court under section *42*, the certificate shall thereupon expire.

(11) A Minister of the Government shall, in each year after the year in which this section comes into operation, cause to be prepared and furnished to the Commissioner a report in writing specifying the number of certificates issued by him or her in the preceding year and the provisions of *section 23* or *24*, as may be appropriate, by virtue of which, pursuant to *section 8*, the grant of the request under *section 7* concerned was refused, or, pursuant to *section 14*, a decision to uphold a decision to refuse to grant, the request under *section 7* concerned was made.

(12) Where a certificate is revoked or has expired and another certificate is not in force in relation to the record concerned or the certificate is annulled under *section 42*, the requester

concerned may make an application for a review under *section 14* or *34*, as may be appropriate, of the decision concerned under *section 8* or *14* not later than 28 days after the date of the revocation, expiration or annulment, as the case may be.

(13) Subject to *subsections (9)* and *(10)*, a certificate shall remain in force for a period of 2 years from the date on which it is signed by the Minister of the Government concerned and shall then expire, but a Minister of the Government may, at any time, issue a certificate under this section in respect of a record in relation to which a certificate had previously been issued unless pursuant to—

(*a*) a decision (which has not been reversed) following a review under *section 14* or *34*, or

(*b*) a decision under *section 42* on an appeal to the High Court,

the record is not an exempt record.

26.—(1) Subject to the provisions of this section, a head shall refuse to grant a request under *section 7* if—   *Information obtained in confidence.*

(*a*) the record concerned contains information given to the public body concerned in confidence and on the understanding that it would be treated by it as confidential (including such information as aforesaid that a person was required by law, or could have been required by the body pursuant to law, to give to the body) and, in the opinion of the head, its disclosure would be likely to prejudice the giving to the body of further similar information from the same person or other persons and it is of importance to the body that such further similar information as aforesaid should continue to be given to the body, or

(*b*) disclosure of the information concerned would constitute a breach of a duty of confidence provided for by a provision of an agreement or enactment (other than a provision specified in *column (3)* of the *Third Schedule* of an enactment specified in that Schedule) or otherwise by law.

(2) *Subsection (1)* shall not apply to a record which is prepared by a head or any other person (being a director, or member of the staff of, a public body or a person who is providing a service for a public body under a contract for services) in the course of the performance of his or her functions unless disclosure of the information concerned would constitute a breach of a duty of confidence that is provided for by an agreement or statute or otherwise by law and is owed to a person other than a public body or head or a director or member of the staff of, a public body or a person who is providing or provided a service for a public body under a contract for services.

(3) Subject to *section 29*, *subsection (1) (a)* shall not apply in relation to a case in which, in the opinion of the head concerned, the public interest would, on balance, be better served by granting than by refusing to grant the request under *section 7* concerned.

27.—(1) Subject to *subsection (2)*, a head shall refuse to grant a request under *section 7* if the record concerned contains—   *Commercially sensitive information.*

(*a*) trade secrets of a person other than the requester concerned,

(*b*) financial, commercial, scientific or technical or other information whose disclosure could reasonably be expected to result in a material financial loss or gain to the person to whom the information relates, or could prejudice the competitive position of that person in the conduct of his or her profession or business or otherwise in his or her occupation, or

(*c*) information whose disclosure could prejudice the conduct or outcome of contractual or other negotiations of the person to whom the information relates.

(2) A head shall grant a request under *section 7* to which *subsection (1)* relates if—

(*a*) the person to whom the record concerned relates consents, in writing or in such other form as may be determined, to access to the record being granted to the requester concerned,

(*b*) information of the same kind as that contained in the record in respect of persons generally or a class of persons that is, having regard to all the circumstances, of significant size, is available to the general public,

(*c*) the record relates only to the requester,

(*d*) information contained in the record was given to the public body concerned by the person to whom it relates and the person was informed on behalf of the body, before its being so given, that the information belongs to a class of information that would or might be made available to the general public, or

(*e*) disclosure of the information concerned is necessary in order to avoid a serious and imminent danger to the life or health of an individual or to the environment.

(3) Subject to *section 29*, *subsection (1)* does not apply in relation to a case in which, in the opinion of the head concerned, the public interest would, on balance, be better served by granting than by refusing to grant the request under *section 7* concerned.

28.—(1) Subject to the provisions of this section, a head shall refuse to grant a request under *section 7* if, in the opinion of the head, access to the record concerned would involve the disclosure of personal information (including personal information relating to a deceased individual).

(2) *Subsection (1)* does not apply if—

(*a*) subject to *subsection (3)*, the information concerned relates to the requester concerned,

(*b*) any individual to whom the information relates consents, in writing or such other form as may be determined, to its disclosure to the requester,

(*c*) information of the same kind as that contained in the record in respect of individuals generally, or a class of individuals that is, having regard to all the circumstances, of significant size, is available to the general public,

(*d*) the information was given to the public body concerned by the individual to whom it relates and the individual was informed on behalf of the body, before its being so given, that the information belongs to a class of information that would or might be made available to the general public, or

(*e*) disclosure of the information is necessary in order to avoid a serious and imminent danger to the life or health of an individual,

but, in a case falling within *paragraph (a)* or *(b)*, the head concerned shall ensure that, before the request under *section 7* concerned is granted, the identity of the requester or, as the case may be, the consent of the individual is established to the satisfaction of the head.

(3) Where a request under *section 7* relates to

(*a*) a record of a medical or psychiatric nature relating to the requester concerned, or

(*b*) a record kept for the purposes of, or obtained in the course of the carrying out of, social work in relation to the requester,

and, in the opinion of the head concerned, disclosure of the information concerned to the requester might be prejudicial to his or her physical or mental health, well-being or emotional condition, the head may decide to refuse to grant the request.

(4) Where, pursuant to *subsection (3)*, a head refuses to grant a request under *section 7*—

(*a*) there shall be included in the notice under *section 8 (1)* in relation to the matter a statement to the effect that, if the requester requests the head to do so, the head will offer access to the record concerned, and keep it available for that purpose, in accordance with *section 8 (3)* to such health professional having expertise in relation to the subject-matter of the record as the requester may specify, and

(*b*) if the requester so requests the head, he or she shall offer access to the record to such health professional as aforesaid, and keep it available for that purpose, in accordance with *section 8 (3)*.

(5) Where, as respects a request under *section 7* the grant of which would, but for this

subsection, fall to be refused under *subsection (1)*, in the opinion of the head concerned, on balance—

    (*a*) the public interest that the request should be granted outweighs the public interest that the right to privacy of the individual to whom the information relates should be upheld, or

    (*b*) the grant of the request would benefit the individual aforesaid,

the head may, subject to *section 29*, grant the request.

    (6) Notwithstanding *subsection (1)*, the Minister may provide by regulations for the grant of a request under *section 7* where—

    (*a*) the individual to whom the record concerned relates belongs to a class specified in the regulations and the requester concerned is the parent or guardian of the individual, or

    (*b*) the individual to whom the record concerned relates is dead and the requester concerned is a member of a class specified in the regulations.

    (7) In this section "health professional" means a medical practitioner, within the meaning of the Medical Practitioners Act, 1978, a registered dentist, within the meaning of the Dentists Act, 1985, or a member of any other class of health worker or social worker standing prescribed, after consultation with such (if any) other Ministers of the Government as the Minister considers appropriate.

    29.—(1) In this section "a request to which this section applies" means a request under *section 7* to which *section 26 (3)* or *27 (3)* applies or to which *section 28 (5)* applies and which, apart from this section, would fall to be granted. Procedure in relation to certain rquests under *section 7* to which *section 26, 27* or *28* applies.

    (2) Subject to *subsection (5)*, before deciding whether to grant a request to which this section applies, a head shall, not later than 2 weeks after the receipt of the request—

    (*a*) if the request is one to which *section 26 (3)* applies, cause the person who gave the information concerned to the public body concerned and, if the head considers it appropriate, the person to whom the information relates, or

    (*b*) if the request is one to which *section 27 (3)* or *28 (5)* applies, cause the person to whom the information relates,

to be notified, in writing or in such other form as may be determined—

        (i)   of the request and that, apart from this section, it falls, in the public interest, to be granted,

        (ii) that the person may, not later than 3 weeks after the receipt of the notification, make submissions to the head in relation to the request, and

        (iii) that the head will consider any such submissions before deciding whether to grant or refuse to grant the request.

    (3) A person who receives a notification under *subsection (2)* may, not later than 3 weeks after such receipt, make submissions to the head concerned in relation to the request to which this section applies referred to in the notification and the head—

    (*a*) shall consider any such submissions so made before deciding whether to grant the request,

    (*b*) shall cause the person to be notified in writing or in such other form as may be determined of the decision, and

    (*c*) if the decision is to grant the request, shall cause to be included in the notification particulars of the right of review of the decision under *section 34*, the procedure governing the exercise of that right and the time limit governing such exercise.

    (4) Subject to *subsection (5)*, a head shall make a decision whether to grant a request to which this section applies, and shall comply with *subsection (3)* in relation thereto, not later than 2 weeks after—

    (*a*) the expiration of the time specified in *subsection (3)*, or

    (*b*) the receipt of submissions under that subsection in relation to the request from those concerned, whichever is the earlier, and *section 8 (1)* shall be construed and shall have effect accordingly.

(5) If, in relation to a request to which this section applies, the head concerned is unable to comply with *subsection (2)*, having taken all reasonable steps to do so, the head shall, if the Commissioner consents to the non-compliance, make a decision whether to grant or refuse the request not later than 7 weeks after the receipt of the request and in such a case *section 8 (1)* shall be construed and shall have effect accordingly.

(6) If, in relation to a request to which this section applies, the Commissioner does not consent, pursuant to *subsection (5)*, to non-compliance with *subsection (2)*, he or she shall direct the head concerned to take specified steps within a specified period for the purpose of complying with *subsection (2)* and if, having taken those steps within that period or such further period as the Commissioner may specify, the head is unable to comply with that subsection, he or she shall, as soon as may be, make a decision whether to grant or refuse the request.

Research and natural resources.

30.—(1) A head may refuse to grant a request under *section 7* if, in the opinion of the head—

    (*a*) the record concerned contains information in relation to research being or to be carried out by or on behalf of a public body and disclosure of the information or its disclosure before the completion of the research would be likely to expose the body, any person who is or will be carrying out the research on behalf of the body or the subject matter of the research to serious disadvantage, or

    (*b*) disclosure of information contained in the record could reasonably be expected to prejudice the well-being of a cultural, heritage or natural resource or a species, or the habitat of a species, of flora or fauna.

(2) *Subsection (1)* does not apply in relation to a case in which, in the opinion of the head concerned, the public interest would, on balance, be better served by granting than by refusing to grant the request under *section 7* concerned.

Financial and economic interests of the State and public bodies.

31.—(1) A head may refuse to grant a request under *section 7* in relation to a record (and, in particular, but without prejudice to the generality otherwise of this subsection, to a record to which *subsection (2)* applies) if, in the opinion of the head—

    (*a*) access to the record could reasonably be expected to have a serious adverse affect on the financial interests of the State or on the ability of the Government to manage the national economy,

    (*b*) premature disclosure of information contained in the record could reasonably be expected to result in undue disturbance of the ordinary course of business generally, or any particular class of business, in the State and access to the record would involve disclosure of the information that would, in all the circumstances, be premature, or

    (*c*) access to the record could reasonably be expected to result in an unwarranted benefit or loss to a person or class of persons.

(2) This subsection applies to a record relating to—

    (*a*) rates of exchange or the currency of the State,

    (*b*) taxes, revenue duties or other sources of income for the State, a local authority or any other public body,

    (*c*) interest rates,

    (*d*) borrowing by or on behalf of the State or a public body,

    (*e*) the regulation or supervision by or on behalf of the State or a public body of the business of banking or insurance or the lending of money or of other financial business or of institutions or other persons carrying on any of the businesses aforesaid,

    (*f*) dealings in securities or foreign currency,

(*g*) the regulation or control by or on behalf of the State or a public body of wages, salaries or prices,

(*h*) proposals in relation to expenditure by or on behalf of the State or a public body including the control, restriction or prohibition of any such expenditure,

(*i*) property held by or on behalf of the State or a public body and transactions or proposed or contemplated transactions involving such property,

(*j*) foreign investment in enterprises in the State,

(*k*) industrial development in the State,

(*l*) trade between persons in the State and persons outside the State,

(*m*) trade secrets or financial, commercial, industrial, scientific or technical information belonging to the State or a public body and is of substantial value or is reasonably likely to be of substantial value,

(*n*) information the disclosure of which could reasonably be expected to affect adversely the competitive position of a public body in relation to activities carried on by it on a commercial basis, or

(*o*) the economic or financial circumstances of a public body.

(3) *Subsection (1)* does not apply in relation to a case in which, in the opinion of the head concerned, the public interest would, on balance, be better served by granting than by refusing to grant the request under *section 7* concerned.

32.—(1) A head shall refuse to grant a request under *section 7* if—

Enactments relating to non-disclosure of records.

(*a*) the disclosure of the record concerned is prohibited by any enactment (other than a provision specified in *column (3)* of the *Third Schedule* of an enactment specified in that Schedule), or

(*b*) the non-disclosure of the record is authorised by any such enactment in certain circumstances and the case is one in which the head would, pursuant to the enactment, refuse to disclose the record.

(2) A joint committee of both Houses of the Oireachtas shall, if authorised in that behalf by both such Houses (and such a committee so authorised is referred to subsequently in this section as "the committee")—

(*a*) review from time to time the operation of any provisions of any enactment that authorise or require the non-disclosure of a record (other than a provision specified in the said *column (3)*) for the purpose of ascertaining whether, having regard to the provisions, purposes and spirit of this Act—

(i) any of those provisions should be amended or repealed, or

(ii) a reference to any of them should be included in the said *column (3)*, and

(*b*) prepare and furnish to each such House a report in writing of the results of the review aforesaid and, if it considers it appropriate to do so, include in the report recommendations in relation to the amendment, repeal or continuance in force of, or the inclusion in the said *column (3)* of a reference to, any of those provisions.

(3) A Minister of the Government shall, in accordance with *subsection (6)*, prepare and furnish to the committee reports in writing—

(*a*) specifying, as respects any enactments that confer functions on that Minister of the Government or on a public body in relation to which functions are vested in that Minister of the Government, any provisions thereof that authorise or require the non-disclosure of a record, and

(*b*) specifying whether, in the opinion of that Minister of the Government and (where appropriate) any such public body, formed having regard to the provisions, purposes and spirit of this Act—

(i) any of the provisions referred to in *paragraph (a)* should be amended, repealed or allowed to continue in force, or

(ii) a reference to any of them should be included in the said *column (3)*, and outlining the reasons for the opinion.

(4) A Minister of the Government shall cause a copy of a report prepared by him or her under *subsection (3)* to be furnished to the Commissioner and to be laid before each House of the Oireachtas.

(5) The Commissioner may, and shall, if so requested by the committee, furnish to the committee his or her opinion and conclusions in relation to a report under *subsection (3)* or any matter contained in or arising out of such a report or any matter relating to or arising out of the operation of this section.

(6) The first report under *subsection (3)* of a Minister of the Government shall be furnished by him or her in accordance with that subsection not later than 12 months after the commencement of this Act and subsequent such reports of that Minister of the Government shall be so furnished not later than 30 days after the fifth anniversary of the day on which the last previous such report by him or her was so furnished.

PART IV

THE INFORMATION COMMISSIONER

Establishment of office of Information Commissioner.
33.—(1) There is hereby established the office of Information Commissioner and the holder of the office shall be known as the Information Commissioner.

(2) The Commissioner shall be independent in the performance of his or her functions.

(3) The appointment of a person to be the Commissioner shall be made by the President on the advice of the Government following a resolution passed by Dáil Éireann and by Seanad Éireann recommending the appointment of the person.

(4) (*a*) Subject to *paragraph (b)*, the provisions of the *Second Schedule* shall have effect in relation to the Commissioner.

(*b*) *Paragraphs 4* and *5* of the *Second Schedule* shall not have effect where the person who holds the office of Commissioner also holds the office of Ombudsman.

(5) *Section 2 (6)* of the Ombudsman Act, 1980 shall not apply to a person who holds the office of Ombudsman and also holds the office of Commissioner.

Review by Commissioner of decisions.
34.—(1) This section applies to—

(*a*) a decision under *section 14*, other than a decision referred to in paragraph (*c*),

(*b*) a decision specified in *paragraph (a)*, (*b*), (*c*), (*d*), (*e*) or (*f*) of *section 14 (1)*,

(*c*) a decision under *section 14*, or a decision under *section 47*, that a fee or deposit exceeding £10 or such other amount (if any) as may stand prescribed for the time being should be charged under *section 47*,

(*d*) a decision under *section 9* to extend the time for the consideration of a request under *section 7*,

(*e*) a decision under *section 11* to defer the giving of access to a record falling within *paragraph (b)* or (*c*) of *subsection (1)* of that section, and

(*f*) a decision on a request to which *section 29* applies,

but excluding—

(i) a decision aforesaid made by the Commissioner in respect of a record held by the Commissioner or (in a case where the same person holds the office of Ombudsman and the office of Commissioner) made by the Ombudsman in respect of a record held by the Ombudsman, and

(ii) a decision referred to in *paragraph (b)*, and a decision under *section 47* referred to in *paragraph (c)*, made by a person to whom the function concerned stood delegated under *section 4* at the time of the making of the decision.

(2) Subject to the provisions of this Act, the Commissioner may, on application to him or her in that behalf, in writing or in such other form as may be determined, by a relevant

person—
>   (*a*) review a decision to which this section applies, and
>   (*b*) following the review, may, as he or she considers appropriate—
>   (*i*) affirm or vary the decision, or
>   (ii) annul the decision and, if appropriate, make such decision in relation to
>   the matter concerned as he or she considers proper,
in accordance with this Act.

(3) A decision under *subsection (2)* shall be made as soon as may be and, in so far as practicable—
>   (*a*) in case the application for the review concerned was made during the period of
>   3 years from the commencement of this Act, not later than 4 months after the
>   receipt by the Commissioner of the application, and
>   (*b*) in case the application for the review was made after the expiration of the period
>   aforesaid, not later than 3 months after the receipt by the Commissioner of the
>   application.

(4) An application under *subsection (2)* shall be made—
>   (*a*) if it relates to a decision specified in *paragraph* (*d*) or (*f*) of *subsection (1)*, not
>   later than 2 weeks after the notification of the decision to the relevant person
>   concerned, and
>   (*b*) if it relates to any other decision specified in that subsection, not later than 6
>   months after the notification of the decision to the relevant person concerned
>   or, in a case in which the Commissioner is of opinion that there are reasonable
>   grounds for extending that period, the expiration of such longer period as he
>   or she may determine.

(5) A person who makes an application under *subsection (2)* may, by notice in writing given to the Commissioner, at any time before a notice under *subsection (10)* in relation to the application is given to the person, withdraw the application, and the Commissioner shall cause a copy of any notice given to him or her under this subsection to be given to the relevant person, or the head, concerned, as may be appropriate, and any other person to whom, in the opinion of the Commissioner, it should be given.

(6) As soon as may be after the receipt by the Commissioner of an application under *subsection (2)*, the Commissioner shall cause a copy of the application to be given to the head concerned, and, as may be appropriate, to the relevant person concerned and, if the Commissioner proposes to review the decision concerned, he or she shall cause the head and the relevant person and any other person who, in the opinion of the Commissioner, should be notified of the proposal to be so notified and, thereupon, the head shall give to the Commissioner particulars, in writing or in such other form as may be determined, of any persons whom he or she has or, in the case of a refusal to grant a request to which *section 29* applies, would, if he or she had intended to grant the request under *section 7* concerned, have notified of the request.

(7) Where an application under *subsection (2)* is made, the Commissioner may at any time endeavour to effect a settlement between the parties concerned of the matter concerned and may for that purpose, notwithstanding *subsection (3)*, suspend, for such period as may be agreed with the parties concerned and, if appropriate, discontinue, the review concerned.

(8) In relation to a proposed review under this section, the head, and the relevant person concerned and any other person who is notified under *subsection (6)* of the review may make submissions (as the Commissioner may determine, in writing or orally or in such other form as may be determined) to the Commissioner in relation to any matter relevant to the review and the Commissioner shall take any such submissions into account for the purposes of the review.

(9) (*a*) The Commissioner may refuse to grant an application under *subsection (2)* or
>   discontinue a review under this section if he or she is or becomes of the opin-
>   ion that—
>   (i)   the application aforesaid or the application to which the review relates
>   ("the application") is frivolous or vexatious,

  (ii) the application does not relate to a decision specified in *subsection (1)*, or

  (iii) the matter to which the application relates is, has been or will be, the subject of another review under this section.

 (*b*) In determining whether to refuse to grant an application under *subsection (2)* or to discontinue a review under this section, the Commissioner shall, subject to the provisions of this Act, act in accordance with his or her own discretion.

(10) Notice, in writing or in such other form as may be determined, of a decision under *subsection (2) (b)*, or of a refusal or discontinuation under *subsection (9)*, and the reasons therefor, shall be given by the Commissioner to—

 (*a*) the head concerned,

 (*b*) the relevant person concerned, and

 (*c*) any other person to whom, in the opinion of the Commissioner, such notice should be given.

(11) (*a*) The notice referred to in *subsection (10)* shall be given as soon as may be after the decision, refusal or discontinuation concerned and, if it relates to a decision under *subsection (2)*, in so far as practicable, within the period specified in *subsection (3)*.

 (*b*) The report of the Commissioner for any year under *section 40* shall specify the number of cases (if any) in that year in which a notice referred to in *subsection (10)* in relation to a decision under *subsection (2) (b)* was not given to a person specified in *subsection (10)* within the appropriate period specified in *paragraph (a)*.

(12) In a review under this section—

 (*a*) a decision to grant a request to which *section 29* applies shall be presumed to have been justified unless the person concerned to whom *subsection (2)* of that section applies shows to the satisfaction of the Commissioner that the decision was not justified, and

 (*b*) a decision to refuse to grant a request under *section 7* shall be presumed not to have been justified unless the head concerned shows to the satisfaction of the Commissioner that the decision was justified.

(13) A decision of the Commissioner following a review under this section shall, where appropriate, specify the period within which effect shall be given to the decision and, in fixing such a period, the Commissioner shall have regard to the desirability, subject to *section 44*, of giving effect to such a decision as soon as may be after compliance in relation thereto with *subsection (11)*.

(14) Subject to the provisions of this Act, a decision under *subsection (2)* shall—

 (*a*) in so far as it is inconsistent with the decision to which this section applies concerned have effect in lieu thereof, and

 (*b*) be binding on the parties concerned.

(15) In this section "relevant person", in relation to a decision specified in *subsection (1)*, means—

 (*a*) the requester concerned and, if the decision is in respect of a request to which *section 29* relates, a person to whom *subsection (2)* of that section applies, or

 (*b*) if the decision is under *section 17* or *18*, the person who made the application concerned under that section.

Requests for further information by Commissioner.

35.—(1) Where—

 (*a*) an application for the review by the Commissioner of

  (i) a decision to refuse to grant a request under *section 7*, or

  (ii) a decision under *section 14* in relation to a decision referred to in *subparagraph (i)*,

  is made under *section 34*, and

 (*b*) the Commissioner considers that the statement of the reasons for the decision referred to in *paragraph (a) (i)* in the notice under *subsection (1)* of *section 8* or of the findings or particulars referred to in *subsection (2) (d) (ii)* of that section in relation to the matter is not adequate,

the Commissioner shall direct the head concerned to furnish to the requester concerned and the Commissioner a statement, in writing or such other form as may be determined, containing any further information in relation to those matters that is in the power or control of the head.

(2) A head shall comply with a direction under this section as soon as may be, but not later than 3 weeks, after its receipt.

36.—(1) The Commissioner shall keep the operation of this Act under review and may, subject to *subsection (2)*, carry out an investigation at any time into the practices and procedures adopted by public bodies generally or any particular public body or public bodies for the purposes of compliance with— [Reiew of operation of Act and investigations by Commissioner.]

    (*a*) the provisions of this Act generally,

    (*b*) any particular provisions of this Act.

(2) The Commissioner shall carry out an investigation under *subsection (1) (a)* in relation to public bodies generally not later than 3 years after the commencement of this Act.

(3) The Commissioner may at any time carry out an investigation into the practices and procedures adopted by public bodies or any particular public body or public bodies for the purposes of enabling persons to exercise the rights conferred by this Act and facilitating such exercise.

(4) The Commissioner may at any time prepare a report, in writing or such other form as may be determined—

    (*a*) of his or her findings and conclusions resulting from the performance of any function under *subsection (1) (2)* or *(3)*, or

    (*b*) on any matter relating to or arising out of the performance of such a function.

(5) The Commissioner shall, if he or she considers it appropriate to do so, cause a copy of a report under this section to be furnished to the Minister and to each public body concerned and shall cause a copy of the report to be appended to the report under *section 40 (1)* prepared next after the preparation of the first-mentioned report.

37.—(1) The Commissioner may, for the purposes of a review under *section 34* or an investigation under *section 36*— [Powers of Commissioner.]

    (*a*) require any person who, in the opinion of the Commissioner, is in possession of information, or has a record in his or her power or control, that, in the opinion of the Commissioner, is relevant to the purposes aforesaid to furnish to the Commissioner any such information or record that is in his or her possession or, as the case may be, power or control and, where appropriate, require the person to attend before him or her for that purpose, and

    (*b*) examine and take copies in any form of, or of extracts from any record that, in the opinion of the Commissioner, is relevant to the review or investigation and for those purposes take possession of any such record, remove it from the premises and retain it in his or her possession for a reasonable period.

(2) The Commissioner may for the purposes of such a review or investigation as aforesaid enter any premises occupied by a public body and there—

    (*a*) require any person found on the premises to furnish him or her with such information in the possession of the person as he or she may reasonably require for the purposes aforesaid and to make available to him or her any record in his or her power or control that, in the opinion of the Commissioner, is relevant to those purposes, and

    (*b*) examine and take copies of, or of extracts from, any record made available to him or her as aforesaid or found on the premises.

(3) Subject to *subsection (4)*, no enactment or rule of law prohibiting or restricting the disclosure or communication of information shall preclude a person from furnishing to the Commissioner any such information or record, as aforesaid.

(4) A person to whom a requirement is addressed under this section shall be entitled to the same immunities and privileges as a witness in a court.

(5) The Commissioner may, if he or she thinks fit, pay to any person who, for the purposes of a review under *section 34*, or an investigation under *section 36*, attends before the Commissioner or furnishes information or a record or other thing to him or her—

      (*a*) sums in respect of travelling and subsistence expenses properly incurred by the person, and

      (*b*) allowances by way of compensation for loss of his or her time,

of such amount as may be determined by the Minister.

(6) Subject to the provisions of this Act, the procedure for conducting a review under *section 34* or an investigation under *section 36* shall be such as the Commissioner considers appropriate in all the circumstances of the case and, without prejudice to the foregoing, shall be as informal as is consistent with the due performance of the functions of the Commissioner.

(7) A person who fails or refuses to comply with a requirement under this section or who hinders or obstructs the Commissioner in the performance of his or her functions under this section shall be guilty of an offence and shall be liable on summary conviction to a fine not exceeding £1,500 or to imprisonment for a term not exceeding 6 months or both.

(8) This section does not apply to a record in respect of which a certificate under *section 25* is in force.

Commissioner to encourage publication of information by public bodies.

38.—The Commissioner shall foster and encourage the publication by public bodies, in addition to the publications provided for by *sections 15* and *16*, of information of relevance or interest to the general public in relation to their activities and functions generally.

Publication of commentaries by Commissioner on practical application, etc. of Act.

39.—The Commissioner may prepare and publish commentaries on the practical application and operation of the provisions, or any particular provisions, of this Act, including commentaries based on the experience of holders of the office of Commissioner in relation to reviews, and decisions following reviews, of such holders under *section 34*.

Reports of Commissioner.

40.—(1) The Commissioner shall, in each year after the year in which this section comes into operation—

      (*a*) prepare a report in relation to his or her activities under this Act in the previous year, and

      (*b*) append to the report a copy of any report furnished to him or her under *section 25 (11)*,

      (*c*) cause copies of the report and of any copy referred to in *paragraph (b)* to be laid before each House of the Oireachtas.

(2) The Commissioner may, if he or she considers it appropriate to do so in the public interest or in the interests of any person, prepare and publish a report in relation to any investigation, or review carried out or other function performed, by him or her under this Act or any matter relating to or arising in the course of such an investigation, review or performance.

PART V

MISCELLANEOUS

Decisions deemed to have been made in certain cases.

41.—(1) Where notice of a decision under *section 8* or *17* is not given to the requester concerned or to the person who made the application concerned under *section 17* before the expiration of the period specified for that purpose in *section 8* or *17*, as the case may be, a decision refusing to grant the request under *section 7* or the application under *section 17* shall be deemed for the purposes of this Act to have been made upon such expiration and to have been made by a person to whom the relevant functions stood delegated under section 4.

(2) Where notice of a decision under *section 14* is not given to the person who made the application concerned under that section before the expiration of the period specified in subsection (4) thereof, a decision affirming the decision to which the application relates shall be deemed for the purposes of this Act to have been made upon such expiration.

(3) Where a statement under *subsection (1)*, or notice of a decision under *subsection (4)*, of *section 18* is not given to the person who made the application under the said subsection (1) concerned before the expiration of the period specified for that purpose in the said *subsection (1)* or *(4)*, as the case may be, a decision refusing to grant the application shall be deemed for the purposes of this Act to have been made upon such expiration and to have been made by a person to whom the relevant functions stood delegated under *section 4*.

42.—(1) A party to a review under *section 34* or any other person affected by the decision of the Commissioner following such a review may appeal to the High Court on a point of law from the decision.

Appeal to High Court.

(2) The requester concerned or any other person affected by—
   (*a*) the issue of a certificate under *section 25*.
   (*b*) a decision, pursuant to *section 8*, to refuse to grant a request under *section 7* in relation to a record the subject of such a certificate, or
   (*c*) a decision, pursuant to *section 14*, to refuse to grant, or to uphold a decision to refuse to grant, such a request,
may appeal to the High Court on a point of law against such issue or from such decision.

(3) A person may appeal to the High Court from—
   (*a*) a decision under *section 14*, or
   (*b*) a decision specified in *paragraph (a)*, *(b)*, *(c)*, *(d)*, *(e)*, *(f)* or *(g)* of *subsection (1)* of that section (other than such a decision made by a person to whom the function stood delegated under *section 4* at the time of the making of the decision),
made by the Commissioner in respect of a record held by the Office of the Commissioner or (in a case where the same person holds the office of Ombudsman and the office of Commissioner) made by the Ombudsman in respect of a record held by the Office of the Ombudsman.

(4) An appeal under *subsection (1)*, *(2)* or *(3)* shall be initiated not later than 4 weeks after notice of the decision concerned was given to the person bringing the appeal.

(5) The Commissioner may refer any question of law arising in a review under *section 34* to the High Court for determination, and the Commissioner may postpone the making of a decision following the review until such time as he or she considers convenient after the determination of the High Court.

(6) (*a*) Where an appeal under this section by a person other than a head is dismissed by the High Court, that Court may, if it considers that the point of law concerned was of exceptional public importance, order that some or all of the costs of the person in relation to the appeal be paid by the public body concerned.
   (*b*) The High Court may order that some or all of the costs of a person (other than a head) in relation to a reference under this section be paid by the public body concerned.

(7) A decision of the High Court following an appeal under *subsection (1)*, *(2)* or *(3)* shall, where appropriate, specify the period within which effect shall be given to the decision.

(8) The decision of the High Court on an appeal or reference under this section shall be final and conclusive.

43.—(1) In proceedings in the High Court under or in relation to this Act, that Court shall take all reasonable precautions to prevent the disclosure to the public or, if appropriate, to a party (other than a head) to the proceedings of—
   (*a*) information contained in an exempt record, or
   (*b*) information as to whether a record exists or does not exist in a case where the

Precautions by High Court and Commissioner against disclosure of certain information.

head concerned is required by this Act not to disclose whether the record exists or does not exist.

(2) Without prejudice to the generality of *subsection (1)*, precautions under that subsection may include—

    (*a*) hearing the whole or part of any such proceedings as aforesaid otherwise than in public,

    (*b*) prohibiting the publication of such information in relation to any such proceedings as it may determine, including information in relation to the parties to the proceedings and the contents of orders made by the High Court in the proceedings, and

    (*c*) examining a record or a copy of a record without giving access or information in relation thereto to a party (other than a head) to the proceedings.

(3) In the performance of his or her functions under this Act, the Commissioner shall take all reasonable precautions (including conducting the whole or part of a review under *section 34* or an investigation under *section 36* otherwise than in public) to prevent the disclosure to the public or, in the case of such a review, to a party (other than a head) to the proceedings concerned of information specified in *paragraph (a)* or *(b)* of *subsection (1)*.

44.—(1) This section applies to—

    (*a*) a decision to grant a request to which *section 29* applies, and

    (*b*) a decision under *section 34*.

(2) Effect shall not be given to a decision to which this section applies before—

    (*a*) the expiration of the time for—

        (i)   making an application for a review of the decision under *section 34*, or

        (ii) bringing an appeal to the High Court from the decision,

    as may be appropriate,

    or

    (*b*) if such an application or appeal is made or brought, the determination or withdrawal thereof,

whichever is the later.

45.—(1) This section applies to—

    (*a*) an act consisting of the grant or the grant in part under *section 8* or by virtue of *section 14* or *34* of a request under *section 7*,

    (*b*) an act consisting of the furnishing to a person under *section 18* of a statement specified in that section, or

    (*c*) an act consisting of the publication under *section 15* or *16* of a document specified in that section,

being an act that was required or authorised by, and complied with the provisions of, this Act or was reasonably believed by the head concerned to have been so required or authorised and to comply with the provisions of this Act.

(2) Subject to the provisions of this section, civil or criminal proceedings shall not lie in any court—

    (*a*) against—

        (i)   the State,

        (ii) a public body,

        (iii) a head,

        (iv) a director or a member of the staff of a public body, or

        (v) a person providing a service for a public body under a contract for services with the body,

    in respect of an act to which this section applies or any consequences of such an act, or

    (*b*) against the author of a record to which an act specified in *subsection (1)(a)* relates or any other person in respect of any publication involved in, or resulting from, that act by reason of that author or other person having supplied the record to the public body.

(3) *Subsection (2)* does not apply in relation to proceedings for breach of a duty imposed by *section 16*.

(4) Civil or criminal proceedings shall not lie in any court against the Commissioner or a member of the staff of the Commissioner in respect of anything said or done in good faith by the Commissioner or member in the course of the performance or purported performance of a function of the Commissioner or member.

(5) The grant of a request under *section 7* shall not be taken as constituting an authorisation or approval—

    (*a*) for the purposes of he law relating to defamation or breach of confidence, of the publication of the record concerned or any information contained therein by the requester concerned or any other person,

    (*b*) for the purposes of the law of copyright, of the doing by the requester concerned of any act comprised within the copyright in—

        (i)   any literary, dramatic, musical or artistic work,

        (ii) any sound recording, cinematograph film, television broadcast or sound broadcast, or

        (iii) a published edition of a literary, dramatic, musical or artistic work, contained in the record concerned, or

    (*c*) for the purposes of the Performers' Protection Act, 1968, of the doing by the requester concerned, in relation to any record or cinematograph film (within the meaning, in each case, of that Act) contained in the record concerned, of an act prohibited by that Act.

(6) Words or expressions that are used in *subparagraph (i)*, *(ii)* or *(iii)* of *subsection (5)(b)* and are also used in the Copyright Act, 1963, have in those subparagraphs the same meanings as in that Act.

46.—(1) This Act does not apply to— Restriction of Act.

    (*a*) a record held by—

        (i)   the courts,

        (ii) a tribunal to which the Tribunals of Inquiry (Evidence) Act, 1921, is applied, or

        (iii) a service tribunal within the meaning of *section 161* of the Defence Act, 1954,

    and relating to, or to proceedings in, a court or such a tribunal other than—

        (I) a record that relates to proceedings in a court or such a tribunal held in public but was not created by the court or tribunal and whose disclosure to the general public is not prohibited by the court or the tribunal, or

        (II) a record relating to the general administration of the courts or the offices of the courts or such a tribunal or any offices of such a tribunal,

    (*b*) a record held or created by the Attorney General or the Director of Public Prosecutions or the Office of the Attorney General or the Director of Public Prosecutions (other than a record concerning the general administration of either of those Offices),

    (*c*) a record relating to—

        (i)   a review under *section 34* or an investigation under *section 36*,

        (ii) an audit, inspection or examination carried out by the Comptroller and Auditor General under the Comptroller and Auditor General Acts, 1923 and 1993, the Exchequer and Audit Department Acts, 1866 and 1921, or any other enactment, or

        (iii) an investigation or examination carried out by the Ombudsman under the Ombudsman Act, 1980, other than—

(I) such a record that was created before the commencement of the review, investigation, audit, inspection or examination aforesaid, or

(II) a record relating to the general administration of the Office of the Commissioner, the Office of the Comptroller and Auditor General or the Office of the Ombudsman,

(d) a record relating to the President,

(e) a record relating to any of the private papers (within the meaning of Article 15.10 of the Constitution) of a member of either House of the Oireachtas or an official document of either or both of such Houses that is required by the rules or standing orders of either or both of such Houses to be treated as confidential, or

(f) a record relating to information whose disclosure could reasonably be expected to reveal or lead to the revelation of—

(i) the identity of a person who has provided information to a public body in confidence in relation to the enforcement of the criminal law, or

(ii) any other source of such information provided in confidence to a public body.

(2) Subject to *subsection (3)*, this Act does not apply to—

(a) a record that is available for inspection by members of the public whether upon payment or free of charge, or

(b) a record a copy of which is available for purchase or removal free of charge by members of the public,

whether by virtue of an enactment (other than this Act) or otherwise.

(3) A record shall not be within *subsection (2)* by reason only of the fact that it contains information constituting personal data to which the Data Protection Act, 1988, applies.

Fees.   **47.**—(1) Subject to the provisions of this section, a fee of such amount as may be appropriate having regard to the provisions of this section shall be charged by the public body concerned and paid by the requester concerned to the body in respect of the grant of a request under *section 7.*

(2) Subject to the provisions of this section, the amount of a fee under this section shall be equal to—

(a) the estimated cost of the search for and retrieval of the record concerned, and

(b) the estimated cost of any copy of the record made by the public body concerned for the requester concerned,

as determined by the head concerned.

(3) For the purposes of *subsection (2)*—

(a) the amount of the cost of the search for and retrieval of a record shall be calculated at the rate of such amount per hour as stands prescribed for the time being in respect of the time that was spent, or ought, in the opinion of the head concerned, to have been spent, by each person concerned in carrying out the search and retrieval efficiently, and

(b) the amount of the cost specified in *subsection (2)(b)* shall not exceed such amount (if any) as stands prescribed for the time being and the determination of that amount shall be in compliance with any provisions standing prescribed for the time being, in relation to such determination.

(4) Where the record or records concerned contains or contain only personal information relating to the requester concerned, then, in calculating the amount of the fee under *subsection (1)*—

(a) *paragraph (a)* of *subsection (2)* shall be disregarded unless the grant concerned relates to a significant number of records, and

(b) *paragraph (b)* of that subsection shall be disregarded if, in the opinion of the head concerned, it would not be reasonable, having regard to the means of the requester and the nature of the record concerned, to include the cost specified in that paragraph in the calculation.

(5) A head may reduce the amount of or waive a fee or deposit under *subsection (1)* or *(7)* if, in his or her opinion, some or all of the information contained in the record concerned would be of particular assistance to the understanding of an issue of national importance.

(6) A fee shall not be charged under *subsection (1)* if, in the opinion of the head concerned, the cost of collecting and accounting for the fee together with any other administrative costs incurred by the public body concerned in relation to the fee would exceed the amount of the fee.

(7) Where, in the opinion of the head concerned, the estimated cost, as determined by the head, of the search for and retrieval of a record the subject of a request under *section 7* is likely to exceed £40 or such other amount as may stand determined for the time being—

  (*a*) a deposit of such amount as may be determined by the head (not being less than 20 per cent of such cost) shall be charged by the public body concerned and paid by the requester concerned to the body,

  (*b*) the process of search for and retrieval of the record shall not be commenced by the body until the deposit has been paid, and

  (*c*) the head shall not later than 2 weeks after the receipt of the request aforesaid, cause a request in writing for payment of the deposit to be given to the requester and the document shall include an estimate of the length of time that the process of searching for and retrieving the record will occupy and a statement that the process will not be begun until the deposit has been paid and that the date on which a decision will be made in relation to the request will be determined by reference to the date of such payment.

(8) In a case to which *subsection (7)* applies, the head concerned shall, if so requested by the requester concerned—

  (*a*) specify to him or her the amendments (if any) to the request under *section 7* concerned that, if made, would have the effect of reducing or eliminating the deposit payable under that subsection, and

  (*b*) if amendments are specified under *paragraph (a)*, make such of them (if any) to the request as the requester may determine.

(9) Where a deposit under *subsection (7)* is paid, the amount of the fee under *subsection (1)* payable in respect of the grant of the request under *section 7* concerned shall be reduced by the amount of the deposit.

(10) Where a deposit under *subsection (7)* is paid and, subsequently, the grant of the request under *section 7* concerned is refused or is granted in relation to a part only of the record concerned, the amount of the deposit or, if a fee under this section is payable in respect of the grant, so much (if any) of that amount as exceeds the amount of the fee shall be repaid to the requester concerned.

(11) Where a fee or deposit under this section is paid and, subsequently, the fee or deposit is annulled or varied under *section 14, 34* or *42*, the amount of the fee or deposit so annulled or, as the case may be, any amount thereof in excess of the amount thereof as so varied shall be repaid to the requester concerned.

(12) *Section 8 (1)* shall be construed and have effect—

  (*a*) in relation to a case in which a deposit is payable under *subsection (7)*, as if the reference to 4 weeks were a reference to a period consisting of 4 weeks together with the period from the giving of the request under *subsection (7)* concerned to the requester concerned to the date of the receipt of the deposit,

  (*b*) in relation to a case in which such a deposit is annulled following a review under *section 14* or *34* or an appeal under *section 42*, as if the reference to 4 weeks were a reference to a period consisting of 4 weeks together with the period from the giving of the request under *subsection (7)* concerned to the requester concerned to the date of the decision under *section 42* or, as the case may be, of the giving to the requester concerned of notice under *section 14* or *34* of the decision, and (*c*) in relation to a case in which an amendment pursuant to *subsection (8)* has the effect of eliminating such a deposit, as if the reference to the receipt of a request under that section were a reference to the making of the amendment.

(13) The Public Offices Fees Act, 1879, shall not apply to fees under this section.

Amendment of Official Secrets Act, 1965.

48.—(1) A person who is, or reasonably believes that he or she is, authorised by this Act to communicate official information to another person shall be deemed for the purposes of section 4 of the Official Secrets Act, 1963, to be duly authorised to communicate that information.

(2) In a prosecution for an offence under *section 5* or *9* of that Act, it shall be a defence to prove that the act to which the charge of the offence relates is authorised, or is reasonably believed by the person charged to be authorised, by this Act.

FIRST SCHEDULE

PUBLIC BODIES

Section 2.

1. Each of the following shall be a public body for the purposes of this Act:
   (1) the Department of Agriculture, Food and Forestry,
       the Department of Arts, Culture and the Gaeltacht,
       the Department of Defence,
       the Department of Education,
       the Department of Enterprise and Employment,
       the Department of the Environment,
       the Department of Equality and Law Reform,
       the Department of Finance,
       the Department of Foreign Affairs,
       the Department of Health,
       the Department of Justice (including the Probation and Welfare Service),
       the Department of the Marine,
       the Department of Social Welfare,
       the Department of the Taoiseach,
       the Department of Tourism and Trade,
       the Department of Transport, Energy and Communications,
       the Office of the Tánaiste,
       the Office of the Attorney General.

   (2) the Army Pensions Board,
       the Blood Transfusion Service Board,
       the Board of the National Library of Ireland,
       the Board of the National Museum of Ireland,
       An Bord Pleanála,
       the Censorship of Publications Board,
       the Central Statistics Office,
       the Civil Service Commissioners,
       An Coimisiún Logainmneacha,
       An Comhairle na Nimheanna,
       An Comhairle na nOspidéal,
       the Commissioners of Charitable Donations and Bequests,
       the Companies Registration Office,
       the Competition Authority,
       the Commissioners of Public Works,

the Defence Forces,
the Employment Equality Agency,
the Environmental Information Service,
the Environmental Protection Agency,
the Government Information Services,
the Heritage Council,
the Ireland–United States Commission for Educational Exchange,
the Irish Manuscripts Commission,
the Irish Medicines Board,
the Irish Sports Council,
the Land Registry,
the Local Appointments Commissioners,
the National Archives,
the National Archives Advisory Council,
the National Council for Curriculum and Assessment,
the National Gallery of Ireland,
the Office of the Appeal Commissioners for the purposes of the Tax Acts,
the Office of the Chief Medical Officer for the Civil Service,
the Office of the Commissioner,
the Office of the Commissioner of Valuation and Boundary Surveyor for Ireland,
the Office of the Comptroller and Auditor General,
the Office of the Director of Consumer Affairs,
the Office of the Director of Public Prosecutions,
the Office of the Houses of the Oireachtas,
the Office of the Official Censor of Films,
the Office of the Ombudsman,
the Office of the Registrar of Friendly Societies,
the Patents Office,
the Pensions Board,
the Public Offices Commission,
the Registry of Deeds,
the Revenue Commissioners,
the Social Welfare Appeals Office,
the State Laboratory.

(3) a local authority.

(4) a health board.

(5) any body, organisation or group standing prescribed for the time being, with the consent of such other (if any) Minister of the Government as the Minister considers appropriate having regard to the functions of that other Minister of the Government, and being—

    (*a*) the Garda Síochána,

    (*b*) a body, organisation or group established—

        (i) by or under any enactment (other than the Companies Acts, 1963 to 1990) or any scheme administered by a Minister of the Government,

        or

        (ii) under the Companies Acts, 1963 to 1990, in pursuance of powers conferred by or under another enactment, and financed wholly or partly, whether directly or indirectly, by means of moneys provided, or loans made or guaranteed, by a Minister of the Government or the issue of shares held by or on behalf of a Minister of the Government,

    (*c*) any other body, organisation or group financed as aforesaid,

    (*d*) a company (within the meaning of the Companies Act, 1963) a majority of the shares in which are held by or on behalf of a Minister of the Government,

    (*e*) any other body, organisation or group appointed by the Government or a Minister of the Government, (*f*) subject to *paragraph 2*, any other body, organisation or group on which functions in relation to the general public or a class of the general public stand conferred by any enactment, or

    (*g*) a subsidiary of a body, organisation or group specified in any of the foregoing provisions of this subparagraph.

2. A body, organisation or group standing prescribed pursuant to regulations for the purposes of *clause (f)* of *paragraph 1 (5)* shall be a public body only as respects functions referred to in that clause.

3. The Minister may, with the consent of such other (if any) Minister of the Government as the Minister considers appropriate having regard to the functions of that other Minister of the Government, by regulations amend *subparagraph (2)* of *paragraph 1* by the deletion of a reference to any public body.

4. A reference in *subparagraph (1)* of *paragraph 1* to any particular Department of State shall be construed as—

    (*a*) including a reference to a body, organisation or group specified in relation to that Department of State in the Schedule to the Ministers and Secretaries Act, 1924 (not being a public body specified in *subparagraph (2)* of that paragraph), and

    (*b*) not including any other body, organisation or group.

SECOND SCHEDULE

THE INFORMATION COMMISSIONER

Section 33.   1. Subject to the provisions of this Schedule, a person appointed to be the Commissioner shall hold the office for a term of 6 years and may be re-appointed to the office for a second or subsequent term.

2. A person appointed to be the Commissioner—

    (*a*) may at his or her own request be relieved of office by the President,

    (*b*) may be removed from office by the President but shall not be removed from office except for stated misbehaviour, incapacity or bankruptcy and then only upon resolutions passed by Dáil Éireann and by Seanad Éireann calling for his or her removal,

    (*c*) shall in any case vacate the office on attaining the age of 67 years.

3. (1) Where a person who holds the office of Commissioner is—

    (*a*) nominated as a member of Seanad Éireann,

    (*b*) elected as a member of either House of the Oireachtas or a local authority or to the European Parliament, or

    (*c*) regarded, pursuant to section 15 (inserted by the European Parliament Elections Act, 1993) of the European Assembly Act, 1977, as having been elected to the European Parliament to fill a vacancy,

he or she shall thereupon cease to be the Commissioner.

(2) A person who is for the time being entitled under the standing orders of either House of the Oireachtas to sit therein or who is a member of the European Parliament or a local authority shall, while he or she is so entitled or is such a member, be disqualified for being appointed to be the Commissioner.

4. A person who holds the office of Commissioner shall not hold any other office or employment in respect of which emoluments are payable or be a member of the Reserve Defence Force.

5. The Commissioner shall be paid, out of moneys provided by the Oireachtas, such remuneration and allowances for expenses as the Minister may from time to time determine.

6. (1) The Minister may make and carry out, in accordance with its terms, a scheme or

schemes for the granting of pensions, gratuities or allowances on retirement or death to, or in respect of, persons who have held the office of Commissioner.

(2) The Minister may at any time make and carry out, in accordance with its terms, a scheme or schemes amending or revoking a scheme under this paragraph.

(3) A scheme under this paragraph shall be laid before each House of the Oireachtas as soon as may be after it is made and, if a resolution annulling the scheme is passed by either such House within the next 21 days on which that House has sat after the scheme is laid before it, the scheme shall be annulled accordingly but without prejudice to the validity of anything previously done thereunder.

7. (1) The Minister may appoint to be members of the staff of the Commissioner such number of persons as the Minister may determine from time to time.

(2) Members of the staff of the Commissioner shall be civil servants in the Civil Service of the State (within the meaning of the Civil Service Regulation Act, 1956).

(3) The Minister may delegate to the Commissioner the powers exercisable by him or her under the Civil Service Commissioners Act, 1956, and the Civil Service Regulation Acts, 1956 and 1958, as the appropriate authority in relation to members of the staff of the Commissioner and, if the Minister does so, then, so long as the delegation remains in force—

> (*a*) those powers shall, in lieu of being exercisable by the Minister be exercisable by the Commissioner, and
>
> (*b*) the Commissioner shall, in lieu of the Minister, be for the purposes of this Act the appropriate authority in relation to members of the staff of the Commissioner.

8. (1) The Commissioner shall keep, in such form as may be approved of by the Minister, all proper and usual accounts of all moneys received or expended by him or her and all such special accounts (if any) as the Minister may direct.

(2) Accounts kept in pursuance of this paragraph in respect of each year shall be submitted by the Commissioner in the following year on a date not later than a date specified by the Minister to the Comptroller and Auditor General for audit and, as soon as may be after the audit, a copy of those accounts, or of such extracts from those accounts as the Minister may specify, together with the report of the Comptroller and Auditor General on the accounts, shall be presented by the Commissioner to the Minister who shall cause copies of the documents presented to him or her to be laid before each House of the Oireachtas.

9. The Commissioner may delegate to a member of the staff of the Commissioner any of the functions of the Commissioner (other than those under this paragraph or *section 40*) and *subsections (2)* to *(4)* of *section 4* shall, with any necessary modifications, have effect for the purposes of a delegation under this paragraph as they have effect for the purposes of a delegation under that section; and references in this Act to the Commissioner shall be construed, where appropriate having regard to any delegation under this paragraph, as including references to any person to whom functions stand delegated by the delegation.

THIRD SCHEDULE

ENACTMENTS EXCLUDED FROM APPLICATION OF *Section 32.*

PART I

STATUTES

Number and Year	Short Title	Provision
No. 26 of 1946	Industrial Relations Act, 1946.	Section 22.
No. 1 of 1963	Official Secrets Act, 1963.	Sections 4, 5 and 9.
No. 14 of 1969	Industrial Relations Act, 1969.	Section 14.
No. 30 of 1976	Gas Act, 1976.	Section 20.
No. 16 of 1977	Employment Equality Act, 1977.	Section 43(5).
No. 5 of 1979	Údardás na Gaeltachta Act, 1979.	Section 15.
No. 36 of 1980	Irish Film Board Act, 1980.	Section 18.
No. 26 of 1983	Postal and Telecommunications Services Act,1983.	Section 37.
No. 28 of 1983	Local Government (Planning and Development) Act, 1983	Section 13.
No. 2 of 1984	National Social Services Board Act, 1984.	Section 16.
No. 9 of 1986	Industrial Development Act, 1986.	Sections 42 and 43.
No. 14 of 1986	Combat Poverty Agency Act, 1986.	Section 20.
No 31 of 1986	Transport (Re-organisation of Córas Iompair Éireann) Act, 1986.	Section 22.
No. 10 of 1987	Labour Services Act, 1987.	Section 13.
No. 31 of 1987	Restrictive Practices (Amendment) Act, 1987.	Section 36.
No. 18 of 1988	Agriculture (Research, Training and Advice) Act, 1988.	Section 14.
No. 26 of 1988	Forestry Act, 1988.	Section 33.
No 7 of 1989	Safety, Health and Welfare at Work Act, 1989.	Section 45.
No. 1 of 1990	Bord Glas Act, 1990.	Section 23.
No. 18 of 1990	National Treasury Management Agency Act, 1990.	Section 14.
No. 19 of 1990	Industrial Relations Act, 1990.	Section 25(6).
No. 25 of 1990	Pensions Act, 1990.	Section 24.
No. 2 of 1991	Marine Institute Act, 1991.	Section 15.
No. 9 of 1991	Radiological Protection Act, 1991.	Section 36(1)(*d*).
No. 22 of 1991	Trade and Marketing Promotion Act, 1991.	Section 10.
No. 24 of 1991	Competition Act, 1991.	Paragraph 9 of Schedule.
No. 7 of 1989	Environmental Protection Agency Act, 1992.	Section 39.
No. 14 of 1993	Roads Act, 1993.	Section 38.
No. 19 of 1993	Industrial Development Act, 1993.	Paragraphs 4 and 5 of Second Schedule.

Number and Year	Short Title	Provision
No. 27 of 1993	Irish Aviation Authority Act, 1993.	Section 35.
No. 18 of 1994	Irish Horseracing Industry Act, 1994.	Section 17.
No. 25 of 1994	Milk (Regulation of Supply) Act, 1994.	Section 16(1).
No. 29 of 1995	Irish Medicines Board Act. 1995.	Section 23.
No. 4 of 1996	Voluntary Health Insurance (Amendment) Act, 1996.	Section 8.
No. 11 of 1996	Harbours Act, 1996.	Section 33.
No. 21 of 1996	An Bord Bia Act, 1916.	Section 26.

PART II

STATUTORY INSTRUMENTS

Number and Year	Short Title	Provision
No. 222 of 1983	Housing (Rent Tribunal) Regulations, 1983.	Article 14(3).
No. 175 of 1983	Fire Services Council (Establishment) Order, 1983.	Article 13.